How to Live
the
Abundant Life

How to Live the Abundant Life

Robert R. Davis

Kingdom Works Publishing

How to Live the Abundant Life
© Copyright 2011, Robert R. Davis

To order this or other Kingdom Works Publishing books. For more information or to contact the author, visit our website at **http://www.kingdomworkspublishing.com**. The publisher offers discounts on this book when ordered in quantity.

Contents

Introduction

Why did I write this book? I believe most Christians have not attained the Abundant Life that Jesus described in St. John 10:10. The main reason for this is Churches are not adequately describing what it is and how to reach it. I am not talking about simply using spiritual clichés. I have heard and read enough hyped up catch-phrases to last me a lifetime. I wanted something real. This book is the result of my search for the overflowing life God promised us.

It is impossible to live the *Abundant Life* without love. Love is the core of Christianity and of God. It is the fulfillment of the Law[1] and the greatest of the virtues.[2] Every precept in this book and every work of our hands must be encapsulated in love. How can we possibly expect to please God without it? In view of that, I do not go over it in this book, because it is a given.

We are triune beings comprising of a soul, spirit and body. Since this is the case, we need to address all three of these areas in order to truly live. The Church naturally stresses the spiritual aspect of mankind. Therefore, I will primarily focus on the mental and physical components of living abundantly.

We must ensure that we take the time to address all three areas of our lives. Otherwise, we will never achieve the abundance Jesus spoke about.

This book uses an ample amount of scriptures fully laid out. So that you can see for yourself what the Bible says and check the scriptures to ensure nothing is used out of context. I like to use the Word of God as the authentication for any assertion. Unless I can prove something in scripture it is merely my opinion. What weight should my or anyone else's opinion carry? It is only what God says that counts.

Only by living in cooperation with God's laws can we attain abundance in our lives. In order to rise to a level of abundant living we must go beyond simple obedience, we must understand God's law. If no one understood the laws of physics and aerodynamics, then we would have never been able to exploit them, to achieve flight. We would still be able to travel, but not as conveniently and quickly as we do today. This is why King Solomon states in Proverbs 4:7, "Wisdom *is* the principal thing; therefore get wisdom: and with all thy getting get understanding."

Without understanding, the Law becomes no more than a giant list of dos and don'ts. But, when we understand the principles behind the laws, we can use them to our advantage. This is what living the Abundant Life is about, applying God's Laws to improve and increase our quality of life.

Chapter 1

Cause and Effect

While the earth remaineth, seedtime and harvest,
and cold and heat, and summer and winter, and day
and night shall not cease.

Genesis 8:22

Religions have many laws and commandments, but there is one fundamental law that governs the world. It is the law of reciprocity. Every living thing on the planet adheres to the law of sowing and reaping, without exception. Reciprocity is the law for all life on this planet, including humans.

This law did not come down from Mount Sinai with Moses, but it is just as important to us, if not more. Universal laws are invariable facts of the physical world. God put these laws into place at the inception of creation for our benefit.

"The law of gravity is not a commandment like *thou shalt not kill*, nor a legislative ruling like pay taxes. The latter two are written by man. They can be changed while the Law of Life is written in the fabric of the universe and cannot be broken."[3]

Reciprocity in the Bible is known as sowing and reaping or seedtime and harvest. It is a universal law. Give and you will receive. It is not a matter of faith in God. You do not have to believe in Him to make it work. Just like the universal law of gravity causes objects with mass to fall to the ground when dropped, it applies to everything on earth. Sowing causes you to reap, unfailingly. If you want to live the Abundant Life, you must adhere to this one vital law.

The law of reciprocity is always in force. If we accept the fact that this law works, then we can use it to generate what we need. The principle of reciprocity is summed up in the golden rule.

> *St. Matthew 7:12 Therefore all things **whatsoever ye would that men should do to you, do ye even so to them:** for this is the law and the prophets.*

Jesus stated that reciprocity is the sum of the law and the prophets. In other words, the whole Old Testament is based on and can be condensed into this single decree.

We must understand that the Purpose of God's Law is not to restrict us, but to put us in the position to receive His blessings. This is why Jesus tells us to love our enemies and to bless them that curse us.[4] Jesus is not trying to turn us into pacifists. He is trying to show us how to experience the *Abundant Life* God has given to all of us. If we repay people an eye for an eye, we will reap some unwanted consequences to our lives because of the principle of cause and effect.

Often, we get hung up on the Rules (Law), the dos, and the don'ts. The problem becomes, we can no longer see the forest, for the trees. If we step back for a moment and look at the reasons behind the Law, then we can see every commandment is for our benefit.

I think we as Christians miss the real point of the law (Moses). Every ordinance and command is given because of sowing and reaping. In Judaism, there are 613 commandments that comprise the Law and every one of them was instituted to get us inline with reciprocity.

The Golden Rule:
Do unto others as you would have them do unto you

The golden rule is based on the teachings of the Old Testament. It looks to the individual, in order to know how to treat others. The problem with it is you only have to treat people as well as you want to be treated. You might not feel that good about yourself, due to a poor self image. So, Jesus eliminates this loophole with His New Testament command to love. The platinum rule as I call it looks to Christ, as an example of how to treat people.

The Platinum Rule:
Love one another, as I have loved you

Whatever we do directly to someone, affects us indirectly. Why, because we are all connected by and to God. This is the basic concept of Karma. This interconnectedness is another reason why Jesus abridged the Law to the *Golden Rule*.

For example, the hand is not directly connected to the foot. If your hand decides that it does not like the foot very much and bangs it with a hammer, what happens? If the hand is cut will the feet refuse to run? This should also be our response to each other. Paul said, "So we, being many, are one body in Christ, and every one members one of another" (Romans 12:5). How do individual members of our body know how to function together? The head controls everything. Christ is our head and He will cause us to respond to each other (If we are sensitive to the Spirit).

What we do affects generations that are yet unborn. For example, if I become an alcoholic and subsequently have children, my descendants may be genetically prone to addiction. Failing to see our connectedness is one big reason individuals and companies continue to pollute the earth.

Cause and Effect can work to our benefit or to our harm. Obedience to God's Laws makes it work to our benefit. Remember the Law was not designed to restrict us, to the contrary. If we walk after the Spirit (The Law within us), then the principle of Cause and Effect will allow us to receive the maximum benefit God has provided. In other words, we will live the Abundant Life Jesus promised us.

Cause and Effect can work to your benefit or to your harm

I think sometimes we paint a picture of God as this benevolent entity who sits in heaven answering our individual prayers, like in the movie *Bruce Almighty*. However, God is wise and all knowing. Even with our limited understanding, answering prayers individually would be a grossly inefficient method to meet the needs of the world. So, God created the universe and everything in it to conform to the primary law of Cause and Effect. This is the principal means to get our needs met.

In the book of Genesis, it states that everything can only produce after its own kind.[5] This is another important aspect of reciprocity. You cannot plant apple seeds and harvest oranges. Likewise, you cannot sow hatred and reap love. Faith filled words produce positive results. Fear filled words produce negative results. Solomon points to this concept in the book of Proverbs.

> *Proverbs 18:21* **Death and life are in the power of the tongue: and they that love it shall eat the fruit thereof.**

But, faith is more than just saying the right words. We cannot attain the blessings of God, simply by suppressing ourselves and speaking biblically correct; although that would be an excellent starting point. We must align our thoughts, words and actions.

> *St. Matthew 18:19 Again I say unto you, That* **if two of you shall agree on earth as touching any thing that they shall ask, it shall be done** *for them of my Father which is in heaven.*

This is the known as the Law of Agreement. Agreement does not just apply to groups of people, but it is also applicable to our thoughts, words and actions. If there is disagreement, the results may be less than desirable. There are, in fact, only three possible outcomes. One you get what you desire. Two you continue to get want you do not want. Three everything cancels out and you do not produce any results.

It is important to note, sowing and reaping is not a one for one proposition. It is a one to many, relationship. The biblical definition of reaping implies a harvest. If you sow a single apple seed and it produces a tree, you will not just get one apple. Understand that God is a God of abundance. This law was set in place for our benefit, but if we sow the wrong things it could be catastrophic to us. This is why God implores us to live holy and righteous lives.

If you want to live the Abundant Life, you must adhere to the Law of Reciprocity

---

Sowing and reaping applies to finances, relationships, business and anything else you can think of that needs a successful outcome. God wants His creation to be victorious in every area of life. The law of reciprocity was set up to ensure that everyone would be fulfilled and successful, without exception.

The fall of man caused us to experience the bad side of reciprocity. Prior to the fall, man was sinless and knew only good. Therefore, he could never sow bad seeds nor could he reap their harvest. Once we became familiar with evil, we began to reap a harvest that set the course of humanity on fire.

After the fall, God gave us laws to realign us to receive the blessings of reciprocity. However, the law was unable to change man's new dual nature of good and evil. Even with the law man was still a sinner.

> *Romans 8:3 **For what the law could not do, in that it was weak through the flesh,** God sending his own Son in the likeness of sinful flesh, and for sin, condemned sin in the flesh.*

Jesus through substitution died for us and we conversely live through Him. Now as believers we have the Holy Spirit to lead and guide us. The Spirit can override the flesh. According to the apostle Paul, "If we walk according to the Spirit, we will not obey the lust of the flesh."[6]

The written law was unable to stop mankind from sinning because it is external to us. However, the Holy Ghost is God's law written upon our hearts. Through the Spirit, the law is now internal and able to keep us from sinning.

The Holy Ghost puts us back into proper alignment with the law of sowing and reaping. As Spirit lead believers we should be continuously reaping a harvest of good things. We should be the most blessed people on the planet. This is supposed to be our testimony and how we draw others to Christ. People should be running to us to find out our secret to success. Sadly, for most of us, this is not our testimony.

> Christians should be the most blessed people on the planet

This is why Peter said, "that the time is come that judgment must begin with us, the Church."[7] God's judgment of the Church is not to condemn it, but to align it to the Word. So, that the blessings of God will be upon us and overtake us.

> *Deuteronomy 28:1 **And it shall come to pass, if thou shalt hearken diligently unto the voice of the LORD thy God, to observe and to do all his commandments** which I command thee this day, that the LORD thy God will set thee on high above all nations of the earth:*

*Deuteronomy 28:2 And **all these blessings shall
come on thee, and overtake thee,** if thou shalt
hearken unto the voice of the LORD thy God.
Deuteronomy 28:3 Blessed shalt thou be in the city,
and blessed shalt thou be in the field.
Deuteronomy 28:4 Blessed shall be the fruit of thy
body, and the fruit of thy ground, and the fruit of thy
cattle, the increase of thy kine, and the flocks of thy
sheep.
Deuteronomy 28:5 Blessed shall be thy basket and
thy store.
Deuteronomy 28:6 Blessed shalt thou be when thou
comest in, and blessed shalt thou be when thou
goest out.*

The blessings described in Deuteronomy chapter 28:1-14 come from obeying the commandments of God. The voice of God (Holy Spirit or the Word) automatically puts us in harmony with the law of reciprocity. But, what happens when we do not heed God's voice? According to Deuteronomy 28:15-68, we will receive the exact opposite of blessings. The list is extensive, 54 verses describing the curses in contrast to 14 verses detailing the blessings. It is not that disobedience yields a larger harvest than obedience, but God wants us to see clearly all the ramifications of sin.

Even with the Holy Spirit, Alexander Pope's famous quote rings true, "To err is human; to forgive is divine." We will still make mistakes. Does this mean that we will suffer the negative effects of reciprocity? Fortunately, Jesus also handled that for us, by giving us grace. Grace is more than free and unmerited favor. It means to pardon. It stops us from receiving the full harvest of our disobedience.

We will not always be able to use grace like a get out of jail free card, but it lessens the consequences of what we have to reap. All of these things should allow us to see the true nature of God. The Lord is full of love and compassion towards us. When we truly comprehend how much God loves us. It becomes clear that the only reason anyone would reject the gospel is because they have been blinded to the truth. The law of sowing and reaping is for our benefit, God has provided a way for us to get whatever we need in life.

Let me digress for a moment. The Bible at its core is a self-help book. So, before we look at all the other components of achieving Abundant Life, we should first look at ourselves. This is precisely why Jesus gives us the following instructions.

> *St. Luke 6:37 Judge not, and ye shall not be judged: condemn not, and ye shall not be condemned: forgive, and ye shall be forgiven:*
> *St. Luke 6:38 Give, and it shall be given unto you; good measure, pressed down, and shaken together, and running over, shall men give into your bosom.*
> **For with the same measure that ye mete withal it shall be measured to you again.**

In this passage, Jesus talks about judgment, condemnation, forgiveness and giving. All of these things have one thing in common. The measure you use will be measured back to you. This is the core of cause and effect.

A lot of people have the mentality of doing just enough to get by in life. Unfortunately, after we get saved many still have this mindset. The problem is just doing enough to get by, will limit God's abundance to barely surviving. Instead of recognizing this for what it is, we will normally blame someone or something else for our lack.

Why is this true? Our brains are wired, so to speak to give us a distorted picture of ourselves, due to personal biases and idiosyncrasies. This often results in us becoming blind to our own faults.

So who do we blame for our lack? More often than not, we blame the Devil. Everything becomes an attack of the enemy. So, we pray. We have every pastor, evangelist and prophet, lay hands on us. The results are the same and we are left frustrated. If the problem is due to cause and effect, then no amount of praying, praising, shouting, declaring or speaking in tongues is going to change the situation. We must see ourselves and change our actions. Stop doing just enough to get by and go the extra mile. This is why the apostle Paul admonishes us to give our all in whatever we do.

> *Colossians 3:23 And **whatsoever ye do, do it heartily, as to the Lord**, and not unto men;*

Adhering to this mindset alone will revolutionize your life and cause you to experience abundance. True success cannot be attained without this trait. Be passionate in whatever you do in life. Give it all you got and success will follow. This is not a fluke, God designed it this way. This is the intent behind Solomon's observation.

> *Proverbs 18:16 A man's gift maketh room for him, and bringeth him before great men.*

There are many gifted people in the world, who do not achieve much. Why? Possessing a gift serves as a clue to what you can do. However, you must work and develop the gift, in order for it attract success to you. If you do not combine Proverbs 18:16 with Colossians 3:23, then you are wasting your talents. This is reminiscent of the old joke, "How do you get to Carnegie Hall? Practice, practice, practice."

Talent alone is not enough. The world is filled with talented people. The first step to getting what you really desire in life is a relentless work ethic. Take a look at any champion or highly successful person and observe how much they hone their craft. Remember, the measure you use will be measured back to you.

Hard work without talent is a shame, but talent without hard work is a tragedy.

Robert Half

Chapter 2

Planting the Seed

---

*Jesus answered and said unto them, Verily I say
unto you, If ye have faith, and doubt not, ye shall
not only do this which is done to the fig tree, but
also if ye shall say unto this mountain, Be thou
removed, and be thou cast into the sea; it shall be
done.*
*And all things, whatsoever ye shall ask in prayer,
believing, ye shall receive.*
                                        St. Matthew 21:21-22

Whatever our need is in the physical realm, we can speak
the solution into existence. This is what Jesus is saying in
the above scripture. Is Christ giving us a blank check? Not
exactly, He was simply revealing how God has already set
up the earth to work for us. That is through the act of
sowing and reaping. Naturally speaking, we sow seeds and
we reap the produce. What does any of this have to do with
praying or speaking things into existence?

The Word is likened to a seed you plant in the ground.
Jesus revealed in the parable of the Sower.

*St. Luke 8:11 Now the parable is this: **The seed is the word of God.***

He said the seed represents the Word of God. How is the seed sown? We sow the seed of the Word through prayer. Petitioning God is not sowing the Word. To petition means so ask, beg or plead. This prayer has its place, but the type of prayer I am referring to, is a declaration of His Word. To declare means to speak out, affirm or to proclaim. Speaking the Word plants it into our mind, as if we took a physical seed and placed it into the ground. How does this work?

Whatever you hear with your ears is passed along and planted into your mind. Have you ever been around someone who is singing or humming a song and later you find it seems to be stuck in your head? You might not even like the tune, but the fact is you heard it. Now, it has been planted in your mind, at least temporarily.

The same is true when we declare God's Word. It is a natural function of the brain. This is why the Bible reveals, "Faith cometh by hearing, and hearing by the word of God."[8] This is a key component to getting what you need in prayer.

Remember we stated earlier, everything can only produce after its own kind. Therefore, your declarations must be tailored to fit your need or desire. For example, if you need healing find a scripture that promises you healing. Then personalize it and proclaim it. Stand on the Word of God and declare it without doubting. Doubt negates the effects of faith. It is like pulling your seed out of the ground. Whatever your need is, find scriptures that address your specific situation and start to declare them.

How many times should you do this? A farmer never plants just one seed, but liberally scatters them by the handful. So my recommendation is repeat your declaration, until you feel confident it has been done in the spiritual realm. Then, begin to thank God for whatever you were asking for as if you received it already. This is akin to watering the seed you planted. Once you have watered (offered thanksgiving) your seed properly, wait patiently for God to give the increase. Let's look a little closer at the seed analogy:

St. John 12:24 Verily, verily, I say unto you, **Except a corn of wheat fall into the ground and die, it abideth alone: but if it die, it bringeth forth much fruit.**

Jesus stated that God is truly glorified when we bear much fruit.[9] In order for a seed to bear fruit, first it must die. Therefore, faith or the Word cannot be the true seed Jesus is referring to, because faith does not die within us nor does the Word. We are the seed or the seed coat to be more exact. A seed consists of three main parts, the seed coat, the endosperm, and the embryo. Of these parts, the embryo is the most important.

1. **Seed Coat**: Our flesh
2. **Embryo**: Faith
3. **Endosperm**: The Initial Word

The seed coat protects the internal parts of the seed during a period called dormancy, prior to germination. Dormancy is a protected state during which a seed "waits" for favorable growing conditions (water, light, temperature). During this time, the endosperm is used as fuel to sustain the seed. Germination (growth) must follow shortly because the embryo cannot survive indefinitely. Likewise, the Word must be followed quickly by action or our faith will die.

Germination usually begins when the embryo (faith) is exposed to water (the Word/Holy Spirit). The water swells the embryo inside, bursting the seed coat and setting growth into motion. When faith expands inside of us, it bursts the seed coat, which is our flesh. Therefore, it is our flesh (seed coat) that must die in order for faith to spring forth and grow within us.[10] This is the death Jesus was referring to in the book of Luke. The death of the flesh is synonymous with renewing the mind.

> St. Luke 9:23 And he said to them all, If any man will come after me, let him deny himself, and **take up his cross daily**, and follow me.

Every word we speak whether it is God's Word or our own, acts like a seed. The soil for our words to take root is our mind or soul. We must not only plant the proper seeds, but we must cultivate the ground of our minds.

Every word we speak acts like a seed

Before we can plant a seed, we must prepare the ground of our minds. When we get saved our spirit is regenerated (born again) immediately, but our body and mind are unaffected.

> Jeremiah 4:3 For thus saith the LORD to the men of Judah and Jerusalem, **Break up your fallow ground**, and sow not among thorns.

In keeping with the seed analogy the prophet Jeremiah instructs us to break up our fallow ground. This is land that is allowed to lie idle during the growing season, without sowing in it. The apostle Paul put it this way, "be ye transformed by the renewing our minds."[11]

If we do not renew our way of thinking, then seeds (the Word) cannot grow as expected. Jesus references this principle in the parable of the Sower.

> *St. Luke 8:11 Now the parable is this:* ***The seed is the word of God.***
> *St. Luke 8:12* ***Those by the way side*** *are they that hear; then cometh the devil, and taketh away the word out of their hearts, lest they should believe and be saved.*
> *St. Luke 8:13* ***They on the rock*** *are they, which, when they hear, receive the word with joy; and these have no root, which for a while believe, and in time of temptation fall away.*
> *St. Luke 8:14* ***And that which fell among thorns*** *are they, which, when they have heard, go forth, and are choked with cares and riches and pleasures of this life, and bring no fruit to perfection.*
> *St. Luke 8:15* ***But that on the good ground*** *are they, which in an honest and good heart, having heard the word, keep it, and bring forth fruit with patience.*

The parable lists four different outcomes of planting a seed. The seed represents the Word. Some words fall by the wayside, some on rocks, some among thorns and some on good ground.

In the first outcome, the Word falls by the wayside because we do not focus on it. It is imperative that we read, study and meditate on the Holy scriptures.

To meditate implies a definite focusing of one's thoughts on something, in order to understand it deeply. It also means to ponder (to weigh) or mutter (repeat to yourself). When we meditate on the Word, it has a chance to become implanted in our unconscious mind.

In the second outcome, the Word falls on rocks. This means it is in our conscious mind, but it has not permeated our sub consciousness. The conscious mind is where we form our logical conclusions. It accepts God and His Laws. It is rational to us that we are spiritual beings, created in His image. We can openly acknowledge that we walk by faith and not by sight. Unfortunately, very few of our actions are based on our conscious brain.

We can know God's Word says, "We are fearfully and wonderfully made."[12] However, if we unconsciously have a poor self-image, we will not act like the King's kid, no matter how well we know the scriptures. Therefore, we must repeat the Word over and over, until it forms a picture in our subconscious. Faith comes through hearing (present tense) the Word of God. **Repetition is critical to planting anything in our subconscious mind.**

For example, if someone sings the chorus to a song, you do not know it is unlikely that it will popup in your mind later. But, if they sing the chorus to a song, you have heard repeatedly, more than likely you will start singing it soon afterwards. What made the difference? It is repetition that causes you to recall the song. You probably thought you had forgotten it, but obviously, it is still planted deep within your mind.

In the third outcome of the Sower, our words fall among thorns because we have failed to break up the fallow ground of our mind. Every thorn should be pulled up before we try to plant anything. Our minds need to be renewed.

"Like a fertile field, the mind will return anything that we plant. Now you might say, if that's true, why don't individuals use their minds more? The answer is quite simple. Our mind comes to us as standard equipment at birth – it's free. Predictably, we place little or no value on that which is given to us for nothing. On the other hand, things that we pay money for, we value. But the paradox is closer to the truth. Everything that is really worthwhile in life comes to us free. Our minds, our souls, our bodies, our hopes, our dreams, our ambitions, our intelligence, our love of family – all these priceless possessions are free!"[13]

We need to replace every negative and unproductive thought (image), with what the Word says about us. This is why the scriptures tell us to think, ponder or meditate on good things.

> *Philippians 4:8 Finally, brethren, **whatsoever things are true**, whatsoever things are **honest**, whatsoever things are **just**, whatsoever things are **pure**, whatsoever things are **lovely**, whatsoever things are of **good report**; if there be **any virtue**, and if there be **any praise**, **think on these things**.*

If we do not renew our minds, the old deeply embedded thoughts and actions will choke out our newly formed faith. This will cause us to lead hypocritical lives, declaring one thing but doing another.

In the last outcome, our words fall on good ground and Jesus said it will yield up to a hundred times more than what was planted. This is what we want. It is the good news of the Gospel.

We receive in direct proportion to what we believe. This is another important component to the Law of Faith. It is the reason Jesus said, "According to your faith be it unto you." The seed of faith grows only in relation to our belief. We see this illustrated in Matthew and Mark's version of *The Sower*. The seed that fell on good ground produced, "some thirty, some sixty and some a hundred fold (times)." So, faith is proportional. It brings to mind another well-known law. One that governs electricity, called Ohm's Law.

The relationship between Voltage, Current and Resistance in any DC electrical circuit was first discovered by the German physicist Georg Ohm, (1787 - 1854). Ohm's law states the current through a conductor between two points is directly proportional to the potential difference or voltage across the two points, and inversely proportional to the resistance between them. Ohms Law is the foundation stone of electronics and electricity.

$$Current, (I) = \frac{Voltage, (V)}{Resistance, (R)}$$

Faith works on exactly the same principle as electricity. The power of the Holy Spirit represents the current (I), the Word of God symbolizes the voltage (V) and our unbelief signifies the amount of resistance (R). The more resistance (unbelief), the less the amount of current (Spirit) will flow.

The apostle John said that God gave the Spirit without measure to Jesus. We have the same Holy Spirit that Jesus had when he walked the earth. The Holy Ghost cannot be reduced in power by dividing it up. Remember Moses and the seventy elders, in the book of Numbers chapter eleven.

God took the Spirit from Moses and gave it to seventy elders, yet Moses never lessened in power.

So, what does John mean when he says, Jesus had the Spirit without measure? Christ had zero resistance (unbelief) in God and His Word. Therefore, the full power of the Holy Spirit could flow through Him at all times. We by our very nature (Adamic) have resistance built in, so to speak. Our endeavor is to minimize the resistance as much as possible, so that the Holy Spirit can flow through us and have His perfect way in our lives.

$$\textbf{Power} = \frac{\textbf{\textit{God's Word}}}{\textbf{\textit{Unbelief}}}$$

Jesus' discourse on the Sower does not end until verse eighteen, but we normally stop at verse fifteen. We should continue reading to insure we are not taking anything out of context.

> *St. Luke 8:16 No man, when he hath lighted a candle, covereth it with a vessel, or putteth it under a bed; but setteth it on a candlestick, that they which enter in may see the light.*
> *St. Luke 8:17 **For nothing is secret, that shall not be made manifest;** neither any thing hid, that shall not be known and come abroad.*
> *St. Luke 8:18 **Take heed therefore how ye hear:** for whosoever hath, to him shall be given; and whosoever hath not, from him shall be taken even that which he seemeth to have.*

What do these verses have to do with planting seeds? In the beginning Jesus was talking about sowing seeds. Here, He switches the focus to reaping the harvest. How is everything done in secret made visible? If you secretly plant apple seeds in your yard, sooner or later everyone will know what was done. Why, because once it grows, the apple tree will be hard to hide. The same principle holds true in our spiritual life.

Jesus sums up His talk by saying, "Take heed how you hear". Notice, He did not say what you hear, but how you hear. Remember, Jesus purposely spoke in parables, so the ungodly would not possess the blessings of the righteous.[14] How you hear means to get understanding. He is giving us an important key to living the *Abundant Life*.

Jesus said, "Whoever has will be given more and to him that does not have, it will be taken away." That seems really unfair. Remember, we are talking about seeds. Jesus is saying, whoever is planting their seeds, more will be given (through reaping). After you reap the harvest more seeds will be in the fruit. Conversely, the person who does not plant their seed, it will be taken away. Meaning it will decompose or rot from lack of use. We commonly say, use it or lose it.

So how do we get the benefits of God? The Lord does not drop blessings out of the heavens, anymore than money grows on trees. We must first prepare the soil of our minds. Actively ensure against our seed falling by the wayside, on rocks or among thorns. Then we can confidently sow the Word of God, by speaking it with our mouths.

God speaks things into existence. Genesis chapter one is full of examples. God speaks and it is. Therefore, we speak and it is. Does that sound impossible? Is it a bit more than we should try to take on?

Proverbs 18:21 **Death and life are in the power of
the tongue:** *and they that love it shall eat the fruit
thereof.*

The book of Genesis declares that mankind was made in
the image and likeness of the Godhead. So, whatever is
essential to God is also inherent to us. Our words are a
creative force, just like the Lord's.

But, just because we have been created in the likeness and
image of the Godhead, does not mean that we have
unquestionably inherited the ability to speak like God. In
the field of genetics, there are dominant and recessive traits
passed on to offspring. What if speaking things into
existence is not a dominate trait? Look at how mankind
was created.

Genesis 2:7 And the LORD **God formed man of
the dust of the ground***, and breathed into his
nostrils the breath of life; and man became a living
soul.*

Since mankind has been created from the ground and the
soil functions by reciprocity, then by default we operate in
the same way. This is akin to the father and mother having
brown eyes, nine times out of ten the child will also have
them.

Not only have we inherited the ability of our Father, to
speak things into existence. Moreover, we can clearly see
that He purposely designed us to function this way, by
forming us from the ground. We have been created to
produce whatever comes from our mouths. Knowledge of
God teaches us how to speak things into being and learning
about the earth helps us to understand why it works.

*St. Mark 11:23 For verily I say unto you, That **whosoever shall say** unto this mountain, Be thou removed, and be thou cast into the sea; and shall not doubt in his heart, but shall believe that those things which he saith shall come to pass; **he shall have whatsoever he saith.***
*St. Mark 11:24 Therefore I say unto you, **What things soever ye desire, when ye pray, believe that ye receive them, and ye shall have them.***

In these scriptures, Jesus is simply revealing what God has already done in us. We have a hard time believing this fact because we have accepted a lie. We believe that only God can speak things into existence. This is why we must renew (reprogram) our minds with the Word of God. Then, our beliefs and actions (the right conditions) will cause our words (the seeds) to create the harvest we need. **This is what makes the Gospel, good news.**

Remember back in Genesis, God gave man total ownership of the earth. He gave man dominion over everything that He created. Jesus came to restore what man lost through sin. He came to realign man's thoughts, words and actions to harmonize with the law of reciprocity. This is the key to the Kingdom.

Thinking, speaking and acting in unity
are the keys to the Kingdom

Christ has given us His authority over every situation and we have the power of the Holy Ghost resident inside of us. This is why we can have what we say. We do not have to beg and plead with God, but we boldly make our declarations in faith. It is the law of reciprocity (sowing and reaping) in action. This is the universal law of life.

Some call it Karma. It is irrelevant what you call it. What matters is learning to work with it.

"Your word is a gift that comes directly from God. Through the word, you express your creative power. It is through the word that you manifest everything. Regardless of what language you speak, your intent manifests through your word. What you dream, what you feel and what you really are, will all be manifested through your word.

Your word is not just a sound or a written symbol. Your word is a force; it is the power you have to express and communicate, to think and thereby to create the events in your life. You can speak. What other animals on the planet can speak? Your word is the most powerful tool you have as a human. However, like a sword with two edges, your word can create the most beautiful dream or your word can destroy everything around you. One edge is the misuse of the word, which creates a living hell. The other edge is the impeccability of the word, which creates beauty, love and heaven on earth."[15]

The Word is the most powerful gift given to mankind

There are four things we need to understand and keep in mind when sowing.

1.   Sowing takes time:

We must remember that reaping does not happen immediately after sowing, it takes time. You cannot pray one time and give up. We cannot do well for a little while and then stop. We must pray and do good things continually. This is why the apostle Paul says, "let us not be weary in well doing: for in due season we shall reap, if we faint not."[16]

James 5:7 **Be patient** *therefore, brethren, unto the coming of the Lord. Behold,* **the husbandman waiteth for the precious fruit of the earth, and hath long patience for it,** *until he receive the early and latter rain.*

2.   Seeds can only produce after their kind:
You cannot plant apple seeds and harvest oranges. Likewise, you cannot continually smoke cigarettes and walk in divine health. Jesus put it this way.

St. Luke 6:43 "No good tree bears bad fruit, nor does a bad tree bear good fruit.
St. Luke 6:44 **Each tree is recognized by its own fruit. People do not pick figs from thorn-bushes, or grapes from briers.** *(NIV)*

3.   Sowing is proportional:
You cannot go around giving quarters and expect God to make you a billionaire.   If you give to others by the spoonful, do not expect to be blessed by the truck load.

2 Corinthians 9:6 But this I say, **He which soweth sparingly shall reap also sparingly; and he which soweth bountifully shall reap also bountifully.**

4.   Sowing depends on the soil:
In the parable of the Sower, some seeds fell by the wayside, some on stony places, some among thorns but only those seeds that fell on good ground produced any fruit. The soil represents your environment. This could be your heart as in the parable. It could be the stock market, your work setting, or the retail market. For this reason, we must sow

our seeds (whatever there are) plenteously, in order for some to fall on good ground.

*St. Matthew 13:8 But other[seed] fell into good ground, and brought forth fruit, **some an hundredfold, some sixtyfold, some thirtyfold.***

36

Chapter 3

Victory over the Flesh

But thanks be to God, which giveth us the victory through our Lord Jesus Christ.
1 Corinthians 15:57

We cannot achieve Abundant Life without having victory, not over the Devil per se, but over ourselves. If we fail in this area of our lives, but we attain success in other areas, we will eventually fall and our successes will become marred.

Look around the world today in both the Church and the secular arenas and you will see powerful people losing everything simply because they could not control their flesh (this includes their mouths). This should be a rarity among the people of God, but unfortunately, it is not. I think Lao Tzu a Chinese philosopher said it best.

Mastering others is strength.
Mastering yourself is true power

If we truly want to live for God, we must learn to master ourselves, there is no way around it. We all know our lives are the greatest testimonies (witness) we can ever give. The apostle Paul made the statement, "If any man [or woman] be in Christ, they are a new creature: old things are passed away; behold all things are become new."[17] Although Paul is stating a spiritual fact, this is seldom a physical reality. More often than not, we find ourselves in the dilemma described in the book of Romans.

> *Romans 7:18 For I know that in me (that is, in my flesh,)dwelleth no good thing: **for to will is present with me; but how to perform that which is good I find not.***
> *Romans 7:19 **For the good that I would I do not: but the evil which I would not, that I do.***
> *Romans 7:20 Now if I do that I would not, it is no more I that do it, but sin that dwelleth in me.*
> *Romans 7:21 **I find then a law, that, when I would do good, evil is present with me.***
> *Romans 7:22 For I delight in the law of God after the inward man:*
> *Romans 7:23 But I see another law in my members, warring against the law of my mind, and bringing me into captivity to the law of sin which is in my members.*
> *Romans 7:24 **O wretched man that I am! who shall deliver me from the body of this death?***

So how do we fix this situation? Do we need an exorcism? Probably not, Paul describes what is happening to us as another law. Anything that consistently happens under specific conditions is considered a law. If we take away the spiritual terminology, Paul would be describing a bad habit. The person in question did not have any issues before they became a Christian, but afterwards, they found it impossible to change their old habits.

> *We are what we repeatedly do. Excellence, then, is not an act, but a habit.*
>
> *– Aristotle*

We can change most habits with a little effort and some determination. But habits can become so ingrained in us that they become strongholds. A stronghold is a fortress or something that is erected to defend a place or position. A fortress is built brick by brick (repetition), just like a habit.

Our deep-seated habits are the demons we need to exorcise, nine times out of ten. We may blame it on the Devil, but often it is just our previously learned tendencies at work. The real problem is that the flesh (old man, ego, Adamic nature) is still full of strength and vitality.

We often fail because we try to correct our behavior to match the Word. This in itself is an effort of the flesh, because we are trying in our own strength. If we could do it, why would Jesus have to go to the cross? We must let God do the work.

Normally, when we make a mistake, three things happen. First, we get a "mistake feeling", that nagging sense that something is wrong. Second, we become anxious, and that anxiety drives us to correct the mistake. Third, when we have corrected the mistake, an automatic gearshift in our brain allows us to move on to the next thought or activity. Then both the "mistake feeling" and the anxiety disappear.[18]

If we cannot change our habits or eliminate our strongholds, we usually attempt to suppress or hide the behavior. In doing so, we are never totally free because we are carrying around guilt and hiding things we hope no one will ever discover. We cannot live abundantly shackled with guilt and shame. So the question becomes. How do we break these habits and strongholds in our lives? The bible describes two methods available to the Christian.

1. **Deliverance** (God does the work for us)
2. **Transformation** (We do the work, with the help of God)

Deliverance is the easiest way by far, because it takes absolutely no effort on our part. When we say someone has been delivered from a habit, it means they have been set free from it. For example, when I got saved, I was automatically delivered from smoking cigarettes (1 ½ pack a day habit). In fact, it took me three days before I realized that I was no longer smoking. I did not pray about it and no one laid hands on me concerning it. It just happened.

Unfortunately, we are not delivered from every habit at the point of salvation. Every other vice I needed to break, took a concerted effort on my part. So, when we do not receive deliverance, we need to be transformed. Transformation happens in the mind, which means we must change our thought process. Biblical transformation is not instantaneous, but it implies a progression of changes.

*Romans 12:2 And be not conformed to this world: but **be ye transformed by the renewing of your mind**, that ye may prove what is that good, and acceptable, and perfect, will of God.*

*Colossians 3:10 And have **put on the new man, which is renewed in knowledge** after the image of him that created him:*

Since it is our minds have to be renewed, it would helpful if we knew something about the how it works. "The most important breakthrough in our understanding of the brain in four hundred years is the discovery of neuroplasticity. Neuroplasticity, sometimes called brain plasticity is a term used by neuroscientists, referring to the brain's ability to change at any age – for better or worse. For years psychologists have told us that personalities cannot be changed, but this is not true. Our brains have an amazing ability to change and form new neural connections that can realign our thinking and ultimately alter who we are."[19]

The old adage, "You can't teach an old dog a new trick" is absolutely false. This fact proves conclusively, "As a man thinketh in his heart, so is he."[20] Now, we know for sure that nothing can hold you back from being what God has called you to be.

Finally, science is confirming what the Bible has been saying all along. This is paramount, because now with the help of science, we can begin to understand the details of how faith works within us. The mystical will give way to the practical, as we begin to see the handiwork of God more clearly.

Research has shown that therapy (cognitive-behavioral therapy) is very effective in treating depression for many patients, as helpful as medication, in some cases.[21] CBT is a combination of behavior therapy and cognitive therapy. The common thread between the two is focusing on "here and now." That is the very definition of faith. Faith is how we access the things of God in the present.

Faith pertains to the present.

Hope deals with the future.

Cognitive-behavioral therapy seeks to focus our thoughts on the present realities and not our past failures. The Bible has the same objective, but it places the power in God and not us. The difference is monumental.

> ### New International Version
> *Philippians 4:6* **Do not be anxious about anything, but in everything,** *by prayer and petition, with thanksgiving,* **present your requests to God.**
> *Philippians 4:7* **And the peace of God,** *which transcends all understanding,* **will guard your hearts and your minds** *in Christ Jesus.*
> *Philippians 4:8* **Finally,** *brothers,* **whatever is true,** *whatever is* **noble,** *whatever is* **right,** *whatever is* **pure,** *whatever is* **lovely,** *whatever is* **admirable—if anything is excellent or praiseworthy—think about such things.**

By trusting God to settle our minds, this automatically removes our anxiety and fear of failure. Since it is God, who gives us His peace that is one less thing we have to worry about. This is the point Jesus was making to all who were weighted down with cares. He said, "Take my yoke upon you, and learn of me; for I am meek and lowly in heart: and ye shall find rest unto your souls. For my yoke is easy, and my burden is light."[22] Although God will guard our hearts and minds, remember we are the ones who are required to focus our thoughts on things that are good.

Natural anxiety cure: Trust in God

Changing our old patterns of thinking will dispel depression and anxiety, but in order to change old habits we need a plan. This is where understanding the brain comes in handy.

We commonly divide the mind into two parts, the conscious and the unconscious. Beliefs are formed in the conscious mind and if the belief is strong enough or repeated enough then it will be reproduced in the unconscious mind (This is not meant to be a comprehensive explanation on how the subconscious works).

Once a belief is moved into the subconscious it becomes stronger. The belief at this point changes to a conviction. This is also how faith works. Reading the Word of God and agreeing with it, is not faith but belief. Only after what we believe moves into our unconscious mind, does it become true faith.

Neuroscientists have shown that the conscious mind provides 5% or less of our cognitive (conscious) activity while we are awake. That means most of our decisions, actions, emotions and behavior depend on the 95% of brain activity that is stored in our unconscious mind.[23] So how do we get things into our subconscious mind?

Two methods naturally come to mind. The first is repetition and the second is visualization. This is certainly not an exhaustive list, but these techniques are familiar to most people.

> *Romans 10:17 So then **faith cometh by hearing**, and hearing by the word of God.*

Notice faith comes through hearing, not from having heard. Adding the "ing" to the word "hear" gives it a present continuous tense. This implies repetition. God expects us to hear His Word on a continual basis, with our inner and

43

outer ears. Hearing with the outer ear comes primarily comes from listening to voice of others. Whereas, hearing with the inner ear requires that we hear our voice speak the Word. Hearing through the inner ear is a more potent method when it comes to the affecting the subconscious.

> *Joshua 1:8* ***This book of the law shall not depart out of thy mouth;*** *but* ***thou shalt meditate therein day and night,*** *that thou mayest observe to do according to all that is written therein: for then thou shalt make thy way prosperous, and then thou shalt have good success.*

God instructs Joshua not to let the law depart from his mouth. **Notice, the Lord did not specify his hands, eyes or his heart (mind), only his mouth.** Therefore, God wanted Joshua to speak the Law from his own lips. This would automatically cause him to hear it with his inner ear and affect his unconscious mind.

Next, God told Joshua to meditate on the Law day and night, in order to become prosperous and successful. In other words, Joshua was supposed to focus his thoughts on the Word of God and to ponder over it. Pondering over the promises of God means to see it in your mind's eye, so to speak. This implies visualization of God's promises.

Clearly, God intends for us to use both repetition and visualization in order to change our conscious beliefs into true faith. Real faith operates from our unconscious mind, not the conscious realm.

> *Psalms 119:11 Thy word have I hid in mine heart, that I might not sin against thee.*

Generally, when the Bible refers to the heart of a person, it is referring to the unconscious mind. So, we must place the Word in our subconscious, in order not to sin against God. "Our life reflects our unconscious programming. This is because the job of the subconscious is to create reality out of its program, that is, to prove the program is true."[24]

Researchers at Harvard Business School, MIT, Princeton, UCLA, and Yale gave a few thousand "honest" people the opportunity to cheat in a set of scientifically controlled experiments. Participants were paid about 50 cents for each correct response to a set of 20 simple math problems that they had five minutes to complete.

In control groups, the answer sheets were graded--on average, the participants correctly answered four problems. But in experimental groups, answer sheets were blindly shredded so that respondents knew that it was impossible for us to tell whether they had answered the questions correctly. In effect, participants could simply lie and receive more money than they had legitimately earned. On average, they claimed to have correctly solved two problems more than they knew they had (six rather than four). That is, given the chance, the majority of people cheated by about 50%. Viewed from a different angle, however, they lied about only two of the 16 problems they did not solve--12.5% of their cheating opportunity.

*The results grew more interesting when we tried to understand the circumstances that influence the degree to which people cheat. **First, we found that the risk of being caught did not change the level of dishonesty.** For example, allowing participants to avoid revealing any sign of possible mischief (for example, by having complete anonymity in how much payment they took) did not affect the average level of cheating among them. **Second, we***

45

found that getting people to contemplate their own standards of honesty (by recalling the Ten Commandments or signing an honor code) eliminated cheating completely.[25]

It is amazing that by simply reading the Ten Commandments or by reading and signing an honor code, every single participant stopped cheating. This phenomenon happened regardless of the people's background, age, ethnicity or religious beliefs. Why did this happen? God has designed the mind to operate this way. So, Joshua's blueprint for victory is also our formula for success.

---

1. Read and Speak the Word continually
2. Meditate or Visualize the Word daily

With obsessions and compulsion, the more you do it, the more you want to do it. In the scientific community, this is known as Hebb's axiom: "Neurons that fire together wire together."

"Each experience we encounter, whether a feeling, a thought, a sensation—and especially those that we are not aware of—is embedded in thousands of neurons that form a network ("net"). Repeated experiences become increasingly embedded in this net, making it easier for the neurons to fire (respond to the experience), and more difficult to unwire or rewire them to respond differently.

This is a good thing when learning the name of a new acquaintance—the net helps us to remember; but not so good when being yelled at repeatedly as a child—the net also remembers this, and has a difficult time knowing how to respond later in life when someone raises their voice with us. Renewing our minds is all about creating new, healthy nets that fire together so they can wire together."[26]

It is essential to understand that it is not what you feel while applying the technique that counts, it is what you do. The goal is not to make the feeling go away; the goal is to delay or stop the action. As long as we are human we will be tempted to sin. Even Jesus was tempted. Victory lies in not succumbing to the temptation. The more you separate the temptation from the sin (cause from the effect), the closer you will be to ultimate victory. Here is why. While it is true that, "Neurons that fire together wire together." The converse is also true, "Neurons that fire apart, wire apart." In other words, the less you do something, the less you are compelled to do it. Science calls it rewiring. The Bible calls it transformation.

So, do not look at the isolated incident of sin, but see the overall picture. Trying to stop cold turkey will make you feel like a failure if you slip. However, attempting to break the pattern of a particular sin, gives you the attitude that it is a process and it will not happen overnight. So, when you do slip it is not catastrophic to your faith. There is no need to wait for Sunday and get in the prayer line. Simply pick yourself up and keep going (repentance is implied).

Let's take smoking, for example. There is no specific prohibition against it. Even so, since the body is considered God's temple, it is holy and care must be given to its treatment. If we follow our formula for success, we would first speak the Word of God and then visualize our success.

1 Corinthians 6:19 What? know ye not that your body is the temple of the Holy Ghost which is in

you, which ye have of God, and ye are not your
own?
1 Corinthians 6:20 For ye are bought with a price:
therefore glorify God in your body, and in your
spirit, which are God's.

<u>Example of speaking the Word:</u>
My body is the temple of the Holy Ghost. It is not mine, but it has been bought with a price. Therefore, I will glorify God with my body and my spirit.

Next visualize yourself under normal circumstance where you would smoke, not smoking and imagine how good that feels. Visualize it in the morning and before you go to sleep. Try to make this the last thing you think about before you drift off to sleep, this will help embed it in your unconscious quicker.

Now that you know how the mind works, use it to your advantage. Try some other helpful strategies.

1. Publicize your goal or resolution
2. Make unpleasant but realistic consequences
3. Use positive reinforcement

By publicizing your intention or resolution you force yourself into a position of action. Your psyche will not be happy with facing possibility of public failure. So, your mind will automatically push you to success.

Baptism in biblical times served as a public testimony of your conversion. The focal point of a town was the river or local water source. Everyone naturally gravitated around the water daily. So, when you were baptized, the whole town was aware of your confession.

Today, especially in America, baptism has lost most of its significance as a public witness of your faith. We normally baptize within the confines of our specific Church. This is why it is important for new believers to invite their families and friends to their baptisms. Without a public witness, it becomes easy to turn back to your former state. However, when you realize everyone knows you are a Christian and they are watching you, backsliding is not an option because you do not want to lose face.[27]

> *James 5:16* **Confess your faults one to another,** *and pray one for another, that ye may be healed. The effectual fervent prayer of a righteous man availeth much.*

Public confession causes us to "Toe the line." This is the rationale behind James' admonishment to confess our faults to each other. This also the major reason for water baptism, otherwise we could just wash our feet, hands and head as the apostle Peter indicated in St. John 13:5-10.

The second strategy is making unpleasant but realistic consequences for your actions. If we go back to the example of smoking, we could say every time I slip and smoke a cigarette. I will run a mile. If you like running or exercising, then do something else, like contributing $10.00 to the American Lung Association. Be creative, but make it something that you will actually follow through on.

Last, use positive reinforcement. So, whenever you want to smoke, but do not, reward yourself. It could be a simple as saying something positive. Again, get creative in your thinking.

If we utilize all the tools, God has given us in His Word, combined with the knowledge of how the mind works. We will walk in victory over the flesh in every area of our lives.

Chapter 4

Growing Season

To every thing there is a season, and a time to every purpose under the heaven:
A time to be born, and a time to die; a time to plant, and a time to pluck up that which is planted;
                                        Ecclesiastes 3:1-2

There is a season or time for everything under the heavens. Nature teaches us that after you have prepared your ground and planted your seed, you need to give the seed time to grow. Realistically, you would not plant an apple seed today and expect to be picking apples from the tree tomorrow. But too often we expect our prayers to be answered immediately.

What do you do after you have prayed or declared the Word concerning a matter? Just give thanks to God as if you have already received what you wanted. Sometimes, that just does not cut it. If you are in dire straits, you need to be persistent in your declarations.

St. Luke 18:3 **And there was a widow in that city; and she came unto him, saying, Avenge me of mine adversary.**
St. Luke 18:4 **And he would not for a while:** *but afterward he said within himself, Though I fear not God, nor regard man;*
St. Luke 18:5 **Yet because this widow troubleth me, I will avenge her, lest by her continual coming she weary me.**
St. Luke 18:6 *And the Lord said, Hear what the unjust judge saith.*
St. Luke 18:7 **And shall not God avenge his own elect, which cry day and night unto him, though he bear long with them?**
St. Luke 18:8 **I tell you that he will avenge them speedily.** *Nevertheless when the Son of man cometh, shall he find faith on the earth?*

God is not unjust and we are His elect or chosen ones. He will speedily answer our prayers. Be persistent in your declarations. Be tenacious in your faith, even stubbornly adverse situations will yield. The lesson here is, do not give up. Let's look at another example.

The prophet Daniel was a man who was greatly beloved by the Lord. When he prayed for understanding concerning a vision, God heard him and sent an answer by an angel. Daniel was so intent on receiving an answer that he began a fast. There was no reason to fast because the answer was sent immediately, but Daniel did not know this.

The prophet fasted twenty-one days before the angel appeared to him. The angel explained that the prince of Persia withstood him for three weeks and another angel named Michael came to help him. It is important to note that God did not delay in answering Daniel. There was a spiritual battle taking place in order to stop the answer from arriving.

What would have happened if Daniel had given up hope after seven days? If the prophet said, that God did not answer my prayer. From Daniel's perspective this would have been true, but in reality this was not correct. This is one reason we need to be unrelenting in our prayers. If you really need something from God, then you cannot give up; you must be steadfast and unwavering, to receive your blessing. But if it is not an emergency, you need to be patient. Some things come only with time.

> *James 5:7* ***Be patient therefore****, brethren, unto the coming of the Lord. Behold,* ***the husbandman waiteth*** *for the precious fruit of the earth, and hath long patience for it,* ***until he receive the early and latter rain.***

Water is pertinent to living. So, in the scriptures, the Word is likened as the rain from heaven and the voice of God as the roar of rushing waters. The Bible also speaks of periods of spiritual famine, which is the exact opposite of spiritual rain. It is a period in which the Word of God is not heard (Amos 8:11).

> *Deuteronomy 32:1* ***Give ear****, O ye heavens, and I will speak; and hear, O earth, the words of my mouth.*
> *Deuteronomy 32:2* ***My doctrine shall drop as the rain, my speech shall distil as the dew, as the small rain upon the tender herb, and as the showers upon the grass:***

In biblical times, Israel planted their crops in the fall and harvested in the spring. There were two kinds of rain, the

"Early Rain" which occurred in the autumn and the "Latter Rain", that happened in the spring.

The early rain was the preparatory rain. It was the rain that softened the ground. This autumn rain helped prepare the soil to be plowed so that the seeds could be planted. The latter rain was the cultivating rain. It helped the seeds to grow into a mature plant. So the early rain helped softened the ground so that the seeds could be planted and the latter rain allowed the seeds to bear fruit.

All things considered if you follow these principles, you should always have a harvest. You may have to wait sometimes, because seeds do not produce overnight. Notice, that I said if you follow these steps you should receive a harvest. This is generally true, but it's not going to happen 100% of the time. There will be times when you follow every step and nothing happens. You repeat the process and still nothing.

The Word of God is an incorruptible seed. Therefore, it should be impossible to have a crop failure. However, sometimes you will go years, not months, without seeing any results. So, what is going on? When this happens, God has a specific will to accomplish in you. Meaning it's not the proper season for your harvest yet.

How do you know if it is your season or not? When you have followed faithfully all of the steps we outlined and there are no results for a year or more. A year is not set in stone but I want to delineate between it and a few months. A few of months are a modest amount of time. It is hardly adequate to determine if it your season or not.

Concerning the proper season, let's look at a physical example. I am a native of Connecticut, where it would be unthinkable to plant tomatoes outside during the winter. Even if I broke up the ground and planted my seeds. The ground is cold and will not produce anything. The seeds will die. So, what do you do when it's not your season? This is where we must let patience have her perfect work in us.

Patience is the strength, endurance or fortitude that is required when you are forced to go without something you need or want. Patience is needed whenever you have a calling or prophecy over your life that does not come immediately. Observe what happened to Joseph when God told him through a dream about his future.

When Joseph was seventeen years old, he had a dream that he would be placed over his whole family, including his parents. This prompted an immediate reaction from his siblings. At first, they thought to kill him but Reuben his older brother convinced them not to and they sold Joseph into slavery. So much for the dream, instead of ruling he was now a lowly slave in another country. While being a slave in Egypt, he found favor in his master's house but yet and still he was a servant. No matter, how much Joseph prayed or quoted the Word. He could not realize his dream.

Next, his master's wife falsely accused him of trying to attack her sexually. Here, things go from bad to worse. His master throws him in jail. Depending on what Church you come from Joseph was either in sin or not praying properly. But, was this really the case? Was there sin in Joseph's life? No, sin is never mentioned. Did he follow every step to the prayer formula? Yes. Well, what was the problem? It simply was not his season yet.

While in jail, Joseph found favor with the guards, but we must be real. Prison is prison. At this point, look how far he was from his God ordained dream. Outwardly, he looked defeated, but God had a plan for Joseph. Two of the king's servants were thrown into prison with Joseph. Both had dreams that he interpreted. One would be restored and the other would die. Joseph implored the servant who lived (the chief Butler) to remember him and let Pharaoh know about his plight.

Two long years passed and the butler never mentioned Joseph. Why, the additional two years in jail? Did not poor Joseph already suffer enough? We must understand this was Joseph's attempt to change his situation. Unfortunately, it still was not God's time. One day Pharaoh had a dream no one could interpret and only then did the butler remember Joseph. Now, Joseph's captivity was over, he was released from prison after interpreting the king's dream and he was made second in command over all of Egypt.

Most are familiar with the end of the story. Joseph's family came to Egypt because of the famine and just as he dreamed years earlier he ruled over them. Did Joseph know when his season would be over? It's doubtful. He probably did not discern anything until after he saw Pharaoh and/or interpreted his dream. Likewise, it is unlikely that we will know when to plant. This is why Jesus said, "we need to always pray and not faint (give up)".[28]

Let's do some math. Joseph was 17 years old when he had the dream. He was 30 years old when he began to rule over Egypt. There were seven years of plenty before the seven years of famine. Joseph's family came to Egypt after the famine started, so he was at least 37 years of age when his dream was completely fulfilled. Meaning there were twenty or more long years between the call (dream) of God and the fulfillment. Wow! That blows away today's Christian mentality. How many would stand firm in their faith waiting twenty years for a prophecy to materialize? It seems like a lifetime but God considers this just a season.

> *James 1:4 But **let patience have her perfect work,** **that ye may be** perfect and entire, **wanting nothing**.*

In all of this we must learn to be patient. A seed does not grow into a full-grown plant overnight or even within a year. It goes through a growth process that takes time to happen. We must learn to be patient with ourselves and concerning our faith. We will not become mature Christians instantly; neither will our prayers always yield immediate results. If we are patient, we will reap a harvest and we will not lack.

I believe this case is extreme, but it illustrates perfectly what the apostle James was talking about when he said, "Let patience have her perfect work." Strength, endurance and fortitude are required when it is simply not our season. This will happen to every believer at some point in their Christian walk. Keep praying. Some call it a wilderness experience. Whatever, name you give it patience is definitely required to obtain your victory.

Prolonged waiting for the materialization of our prayers is definitely an obstacle to our faith. During these wilderness experiences, it is extremely important to keep your spirits up. When your prayers and expectations go unmet for long periods of time, you can become frustrated, depressed and despondent. The enemy will then have a chance to devour you.

Your natural inclination will be to separate from others, but stay in fellowship. Push past your flesh, because this is essential for your spiritual well being. You should separate yourself in a spiritual sense and use the time for consecration unto God. Immerse yourself in prayer, reading or studying the Word. Meditate on the scriptures, since these times are preparation (early rain) to bring you to another level of growth. Without the early and latter rains (saturation in the Word) you cannot receive your harvest. You must preserve (pray and not faint) in order to receive the realization of your blessings. Remember, it's growing season and even in this time God has a plan for you.

Chapter 5

Abundant Life

---

*The thief cometh not, but for to steal, and to kill,
and to destroy:* **I am come that they might have
life, and that they might have it more abundantly.**
St. John 10:10

Jesus Christ came in order to give us life and that more
abundantly. Since that was the purpose of His first advent,
we should thoroughly understand it. What is abundant life?
Is it better living or a richer fuller life? The definition is a
little vague in the Church world. The word *Abundant*
means, plentiful, overflowing, rich or profuse and the word
Life is defined as, not just existence, but vitality, energy,
spirit, dynamism. When I put the words together I get,
overflowing dynamism. Dynamism is an expansionist
quality; a policy or practice of expansion and it is
essentially territorial. Dynamism in essence means growth.

Abundant life is closely related to the Kingdom of God.
Jesus said the Kingdom was within us, but a Kingdom is a
territory not a person. People are considered subjects or
citizens. So, how is the Kingdom in us? Abundant Life
causes us to expand continually, especially in the physical
area. No, I am not talking about our waistlines. I am

referring to territory. This means your corner of the world. As God's people, everything that we possess automatically becomes part of His Kingdom. So the more we expand, the larger the territory of God becomes. The scriptures bear witness to this fact.

The Kingdom of Israel

*Isaiah 54:2 **Enlarge the place of thy tent,** and let them stretch forth the curtains of thine habitations: spare not, lengthen thy cords, and strengthen thy stakes;*
*Isaiah 54:3 **For thou shalt break forth on the right hand and on the left**; and thy seed shall inherit the Gentiles, and make the desolate cities to be inhabited.*

The Kingdom of God

*Isaiah 9:7 **Of the increase of his government and peace there shall be no end,** upon the throne of David, and upon his kingdom, to order it, and to establish it with judgment and with justice from henceforth even for ever. The zeal of the LORD of hosts will perform this.*

Israel was told to enlarge the place of their tent. In other words, they were told to make their dwelling place bigger. God told them to spread out to the right and left, because their descendants would eventually overthrow the nations and settle in the abandoned cities.

Abundant Life – is the Kingdom of God in us that is continually overflowing and expanding

---

Believers have also been commissioned to enlarge their tent. Isaiah chapter nine states that Christ's government or rule will never stop increasing. As we make new disciples, they start to live the abundant life (dynamism). Consequently, the Kingdom of God expands and the cycle is repeated. This is how the increase of His government, will have no end.

The Goal
of the
Church

The Kingdom Of God

The Great Commission

To make new disciples fulfilling ...

Have each disciple grow and live the ...

Continually expand yourself and increase ...

Abundant Life

The growth of the Kingdom is directly related to how much people are living the abundant life. If we are fulfilling the Great Commission and gaining new disciples, but the people are not living abundantly, then the Kingdom is stagnant. So, the Church can grow without increasing God's Kingdom. It is critical that we teach believers how to live the abundant life.

Church growth does not equal Kingdom growth

Church growth depends on gaining new members, ideally ones that tithe. The focus in the Church has become what attracts groups of people to the ministry. But, Kingdom growth depends on believers living the abundant life. The focus is on the individual's personal growth which takes more time and effort. Do not get me wrong the two are not diametrically opposed. On the contrary, the Church must keep an eye on both things. The key is prioritization.

Although Church growth does not always lead to Kingdom expansion, a believer's growth (abundant life) leads to not only to Kingdom enlargement, but to the increase of the Church.

Let me be clear, the Great Commission has always been the mandate for the Church. I am not suggesting that we change it in any way, shape or form. The question is what is the best method to carry out that mandate?

In the Church's infancy, undoubtedly street witnessing was the number one method for fulfilling the Lord's commission. However, Christianity is not a new religion. The Church has matured and standing on the corners witnessing and preaching is no longer very effective, at least not in the United States.

The greatest witness we can have for Christ today is our conduct. This is why the apostles had to wait to be filled with the Holy Ghost on the day of Pentecost, before they could be witnesses.

> *Acts 1:8* ***But ye shall receive power, after that the Holy Ghost is come upon you: and ye shall be witnesses unto me*** *both in Jerusalem, and in all*

Judaea, and in Samaria, and unto the uttermost part of the earth.

Prior to this time Jesus gave the apostles authority to heal the sick and to cast out demons (St. Mark 6:13, St. Luke 10:9). Jesus never took this authority away from them. So, if they could already heal the sick and drive out demons, what power did they need before they could be witnesses?

The apostles needed the power of the Holy Spirit, to transform their lives. Only when the Spirit is leading us can we be effective witnesses for the Lord, because it is through Him that we can override the flesh.

As I said earlier, the written law was unable to stop mankind from sinning because it is external to us. But, the Holy Ghost is God's law written upon our hearts. Through the Spirit, the law is now internal and able to keep us from sinning. The Spirit puts us back into proper alignment with the law of reciprocity and gives us the ability to live abundantly.

I believe the best method to fulfill the Great Commission is to get believers to understand and live the *Abundant Life*. As we expand and grow spiritually, mentally and materially, others will naturally be drawn to us. The world will want to know the secret to our success.

God intends for people to be drawn to His Church because of its achievements. This is why we are called to be the head and not the tail, above and not beneath.[29] Jesus put it this way, "we are the salt of the earth and the light of the world."[30] Isaiah and Micah prophesied that in our time, people would gravitate towards the Church.

*Isaiah 2:2 And it shall come to pass **in the last***
***days**, that the mountain of **the LORD'S house** shall*
*be established in the top of the mountains, and **shall***
be exalted** above the hills; **and all nations shall
flow unto it.

This scripture is not referring to the future. The last days have been in effect, since the inception of the Church. Why will the nations flow or gravitate to the house of the Lord? It is because of overcoming quality of God's people. How they react in times of trouble and the way they always seem to come out on top, no matter what. In other words, it is because they are living the *Abundant Life*.

The Church is meant to be one of the most successful entities in the world. We are called to excel spiritually, mentally, physically and materially. The world will beat a path to your doorway, if it has been proven that you can pray and get an answer.

King Solomon was a good example drawing people from all backgrounds because of his wisdom and his wealth. We may not always be healthy, but we should be people known for healing. God has always blessed His people. Look at how Israel left Egypt.

Exodus 3:21 And I will give this people favour in
the sight of the Egyptians: and it shall come to pass,
*that, when ye go, **ye shall not go empty**:*
Exodus 3:22 But every woman shall borrow of her
neighbour, and of her that sojourneth in her house,
***jewels of silver, and jewels of gold, and raiment**:*
and ye shall put them upon your sons, and upon
*your daughters; and **ye shall spoil** [plunder] **the***
***Egyptians**.*

Israelites were slaves in Egypt and consequently did not own anything, they were poor. Yet, when God delivered them, they departed with an abundance of gold, silver and clothing. Subsequently, when Moses took an offering in the wilderness for the tabernacle, he had to stop the people from giving because of the excess. As they entered the Promised Land, Israel increased in wealth and power and the surrounding nations took note of it.

We are called to excel spiritually, mentally, physically and materially

---

Abundant life is our heritage and our calling, but in order to live abundantly we must first understand what it entails and second we must have goals. The Lord will enable us to succeed, but we still have to have the vision, drive and action to make it happen.

> *Proverbs 29:18* **Where there is no vision, the people perish:**

We normally associate this scripture with the Church and consequently, the vision belongs to the Pastor. Often, it is used to stop division from breaking out within the local Church. However, this scripture also applies to the individual. Unfortunately, we normally do not talk about that aspect of it. If we are going to live the abundant life, we must have a vision.

People do not physically die without have a vision or goal. They languish. In other words, they become the walking dead, stuck in a religious rut. God does not want us simply going through the motions. He wants us to be fervent (red hot) in our Christian walk.

Everyone needs a personal vision for their life. It does not have to be spiritual or religious in nature, because whatever you do in life should give glory to God. Dream big and pursue what is in your heart. The book of Proverbs reveals that hope deferred makes the heart sick.[31] So do not put your dreams off. Jesus said, "Ask and you will receive that your joy may be made full."[32]

> *St. Matthew 21:22 And **all things, whatsoever ye shall ask in prayer, believing, ye shall receive.***

Christ declared, "Whatever you ask, believe it and you will receive it." He has given us the key to living the abundant life. So, if we are not continually expanding our territory, either we are not asking, we do not believe or we have given up too soon. We have the right to hold God to His Word.

> *1 Thessalonians 5:21 **Prove all things**; hold fast that which is good.*

If the promises are not true or do not work, then why are we holding on to them? But, if they are legitimate, our lives should be a personal demonstration of the Word of God.

The Church is meant to be one of the most successful entities in the world

---

God is not dropping money out of the sky into our bank accounts. Even thought the Bible says, "I will open up the windows of heaven and pour you out a blessing that you will not have room enough to receive."[33] We know that this language is figurative, but still many act as if God is

66

going to intervene and miraculously bless them financially or materially because of their tithing.

> *Deuteronomy 8:18 But thou shalt remember the* **LORD thy God: for it is he that giveth thee power to get wealth**, *that he may establish his covenant which he sware unto thy fathers, as it is this day.*

The Bible does not say that God makes us wealthy. It says that He gives us the power to get wealth. In other words, God gives us the ability to create streams of revenue. When Israel gave their tithes in obedience, the Lord blessed their endeavors (the works of their hands). If the Israelites did not continually expand their territory, God could only bless them in proportion to what they already had.

In order to be blessed so much that we do not have room to receive it, we must expand. God can only bless us to the level that we can receive. For example, an eight-ounce glass can only hold eight ounces of liquid. No matter how much I continue to pour, in the end, the maximum amount I can hold is eight ounces.

If we want the blessing of Malachi 3:10 (the Abundant Life), then we must enlarge, expand or increase in some area of our lives. Following the previous example, God wants us to produce a twelve or sixteen-ounce glass. By doing this, He will fill it and we will have more than we had room to receive, previously. This is the plan of God and His Laws operate according to it. If you want more, then you must increase.

The Bible and correspondingly this book, gives you the principles for living the Abundant Life. This is not a set formula per se. Everyone is unique and their situation, talents and aspirations are different. So, giving you seven steps to Abundant Life would not work.

If you apply the principles or the laws that God has set in place and apply them to your individual needs, you will be blessed automatically. That is the beauty of it. A law does not work for some and not for others. It works for everyone without exception. Peter discovered this truth and said, "God is no respecter of persons."[34]

Since this is the case we must understand and act in accordance with God's Law (universal). Begging, pleading and petitioning the Lord does little in this area, because He has already blessed us with *Abundant Life* via the spiritual laws previously put in place.

A while back, my wife and I were having a conversation and she asked me, if I did not reach my writing and ministry goals would I be okay with that? She knew I was frustrated at the time. I told her that I honestly did not know. I felt the answer was supposed to be yes, but that was not in my heart. I wrestled with the question for a time. Finally, I came to the realization God designed us to stretch ourselves and expand. Anything else goes against our nature and God's will for our lives. I can hear some saying, what about Paul's admonishments on contentment?

*Philippians 4:11 Not that I speak in respect of want: for **I have learned, in whatsoever state I am, therewith to be content.***

*1 Timothy 6:6 **But godliness with contentment is great gain.***
1 Timothy 6:7 For we brought nothing into this world, and it is certain we can carry nothing out.

*1 Timothy 6:8 **And having food and raiment let us be therewith content.***
1 Timothy 6:9 But they that will be rich fall into temptation and a snare, and into many foolish and hurtful lusts, which drown men in destruction and perdition.

In the book of Philippians Paul is referring to cyclical nature of life. He was talking about the temporary instances, not the permanent condition. Paul is, in essence, saying that he is not moved or bothered by the circumstances of life. Contentment in this case is really stability in our walk with Christ, regardless of our current situation.

Now let's look at the book of Timothy, at first Paul appears to be talking about being satisfied with whatever we have in life. This, however, is not the case. He is speaking against covetousness and greed. To covet is to desire what belongs to another inordinately and greed is a selfish, excessive desire for more of something than is needed. The apostle is warning the Church through Timothy about the consequences of these vices.

Think about it. Was Israel content in Egypt as slaves? Was Hannah content being barren? Was Hezekiah content with the words of the prophet concerning his impeding death? In all of these questions the answer is irrefutably no. Then why should we be content with whatever life throws our way?

> God designed us to stretch and expand ourselves continually

So, am I going to be okay with not reaching my writing and ministry goals? No, I will not. That does not mean I can afford to be inflexible in my goals. The point is you and I should always strive for new ways to grow and stretch ourselves. Contentment in this context equates to stagnation or death. Growth of anything normally includes reproduction. To propagate means to spread out and affect a greater number or a larger area. This definition accurately describes *Abundant Life*. It is important to note, this is God's first command to mankind.

> *Genesis 1:27 So God created man in his own image, in the image of God created he him; male and female created he them.*
> *Genesis 1:28 And **God blessed them, and God said unto them, Be fruitful, and multiply**, and replenish the earth, and subdue it: and have dominion over the fish of the sea, and over the fowl of the air, and over every living thing that moveth upon the earth.*

We normally regulate the command to be fruitful and multiply to sexual reproduction, but it extends to every area of our lives. Long before Jesus came to give us Abundant Life, God commanded us to live that way. So, living any other way is in direct violation of God's Law. In other words, if you are not living life abundantly, you are, in fact, sinning. How does that concept fit into your current theology?

Chapter 6

The Thief

The thief cometh not, but for to steal, and to kill,
and to destroy: I am come that they might have life,
and that they might have it more abundantly.
                                                    St. John 10:10

In the previous chapter, we looked at the latter half of St. John 10:10, the *Abundant Life* that Jesus came to give us. In this chapter, we will focus on the first part of the same verse, the actions of the thief.

According to Jesus, the thief comes to do three things.

1. **Steal** –to take from another without right or without detection
2. **Kill** – to destroy the vital or essential quality of something
3. **Destroy** - to ruin the structure, organic existence, or condition of something

The Parable of the Sower we looked at earlier in chapter two directly correlates to St. John 10:10.

St. John 10:10	Parable of the Sower
Steal	From The Way Side
Kill	With Stony Ground
Destroy	By Thorns
Abundant Life	Good Ground

First, what does the thief come to steal? If we look at the parable of *the Sower*, we will see that the thief comes to steal the Word from our hearts (mind). Put another way the thief comes to steal our faith.

The parable of *the Sower* is found in three of the four gospels. I will take a look at all of them, so we can gain a comprehensive understanding of what Jesus is saying to us.

*St. Luke 8:12 Those by the way side are they that hear; then cometh **the devil, and taketh away the word out of their hearts**, lest they should believe and be saved.*

*St. Matthew 13:19 When any one **heareth the word** of the kingdom, **and understandeth it not, then cometh the wicked one, and catcheth away that which was sown in his heart**. This is he which received seed by the way side.*

*St. Mark 4:15 And these are they by the way side, where the word is sown; but when they have heard, **Satan cometh immediately, and taketh away the word** that was sown in their hearts.*

The thief who steals our faith is Satan or the *Wicked One*. He takes or catches the Word from our hearts, which is to say our minds. How does he accomplish this? The book of St. Matthew asserts that it happens through our lack of understanding. You cannot accomplish what you do not understand. It's like trying to solve an algebraic problem without understanding algebra. Lastly, St. Mark says that

Satan comes immediately. Jesus is subtly warning us about being distracted. Even if you understand the Word, but do not take time to meditate on it and find some practical application for your life, you will not remember it for very long.

I hear and I forget

I see and I remember

I do and I understand

~ Confucius ~

The preventative measure to guard the Word (our faith) from getting stolen is to keep it before you, by writing it down and reviewing it. I am not talking about writing down everything, just the golden nuggets you get from the Holy Ghost and meditate on them.

Second, what does the thief come to kill? The thief comes to kill our joy.

*St. Luke 8:13 They on the rock are they, which, when they hear, **receive the word with joy; and these have no root**, which for a while believe, and in **time of temptation fall away.***

*St. Matthew 13:20 But he that received the seed into stony places, the same is he that heareth the word, and anon [at once, immediately] **with joy receiveth it**;*
*St. Matthew 13:21 Yet hath he not root in himself, but dureth for a while: for when **tribulation or persecution ariseth because of the word**, by and by he is offended.*

St. Mark 4:16 And these are they likewise which are sown on stony ground; who, when they have heard the word, immediately **receive it with gladness;**
St. Mark 4:17 And have no root in themselves, and so endure but for a time: afterward, when **affliction or persecution ariseth for the word's sake,** *immediately they are offended.*

Looking at all the versions of this parable, the thief employs four methods to kill our joy, in no particular order.

The first method of killing our joy is by temptation. Does temptation really kill our joy? The apostle James phrased it this way, "But every man is tempted, when he is drawn away of his own lust, and enticed. Then when lust hath conceived, it bringeth forth sin: and sin, when it is finished, bringeth forth death."[35]

The second method of killing our joy is from Tribulation. Tribulation is distress or suffering from a trying experience. These experiences should turn us to God, but often they have the opposite effect. Why? I believe it is due to our belief system. Like the book of Job, we believe that we should experience mostly good. But, Jesus said in this world we will have tribulation.[36] The apostle Paul added, "We must [go] through much tribulation [to] enter into the kingdom of God."[37]

The third method of killing our joy is by persecution. Persecution differs from tribulation, in the source of the trouble. Tribulation stems from circumstances and situations, whereas persecution comes from people.

The last method of killing our joy is from afflictions. Affliction also differs from persecution and tribulation, in its source. Affliction is generally from within, while the

74

others are external. Long-term and persistent pain, distress or sickness, will normally cause us to question our faith and thereby kill our joy.

The preventative measure to stop your joy from being killed is to watch what you say. When the pressures of life start to mount, guard your tongue; because out of the abundance of the heart,[38] the mouth speaks and we know that the power of life and death are in the tongue.[39] If you are feeling low or the pressures of life are getting to you, dig into the Word; because Faith comes by hearing the Word of God.[40]

The thief this time is not the Devil. Satan cannot directly kill our joy, so he entices us to do it.

Last, what does the thief come to destroy? The thief comes to destroy our fruit.

*St. Luke 8:14 And that which fell among thorns are they, which, when they have heard, go forth, and **are choked with cares and riches and pleasures of this life, and bring no fruit to perfection.***

*St. Matthew 13:22 He also that received seed among the thorns is he that heareth the word; and **the care of this world, and the deceitfulness of riches, choke the word, and he becometh unfruitful.***

St. Mark 4:18 And these are they which are sown among thorns; such as hear the word,
*St. Mark 4:19 And **the cares of this world, and the deceitfulness of riches, and the lusts of other things entering in, choke the word, and it becometh unfruitful.***

First, we should define the meaning of fruit. Fruit is not one of the nine attributes listed in the book of Galatians chapter five, as the Fruit of the Spirit. This spiritual fruit should be part of everything that we do. Fruit is the product of plant growth.

Initially, we planted the seed, which was the Word of God. After that we continued to believe and spoke life over the seed, so that it took root in our hearts. Now, fruit is the product or result of whatever we planted in faith from the beginning. In other words, fruit is our answered prayers.

The thief again employs four methods to destroy our fruit, in no particular sequence. Numerically, four represents the world and the things that pertain to this life.[41]

The first method the thief uses to destroy our fruit is the *Cares of this World.* We become preoccupied with the obligations of life. As adults we must act responsibly towards our obligations, but we must not let them own or consume us. Jesus instructed us to seek first the Kingdom or God and all of these others things will be added to us.[42] God does not want us to ignore our responsibilities, but He expects us to prioritize them.

The second method the thief uses to destroy our fruit is the *Deceitfulness of Riches.* The book of Ecclesiastes states, "Money answereth all things."[43] We do not need the wisdom of Solomon to know that statement is not entirely true. Just look at people with money and you will see that money cannot buy lasting happiness, joy or love. We are deceived when we believe riches are the ultimate thing to pursue. Since I started with Solomon, I will end with him. The book of Proverbs tells us what the most important thing is and what to seek after, "Wisdom is the principal

76

thing; therefore, get wisdom: and with all thy getting get understanding."[44]

The third method the thief uses to destroy our fruit is the *Pleasures of Life*. Living a life of self-gratification, rather than denial for others will only give us temporary satisfaction. God said from the beginning, "It is not good for the man to be alone."[45] Meaning humans are meant to be social beings. We can only be truly fulfilled when we include others. If you have a really good meal or see a movie that you think is the best ever, what is the first thing you will do? You will naturally want to tell someone else about it. You have to share it, in order to feel completely satisfied about the experience. So living solely for personal pleasure is vain or empty.

The last method the thief employs to destroy our fruit is the *Lusts of Other Things*. For all that is in the world, the lust of the flesh, and the lust of the eyes, and the pride of life, is not of the Father, but is of the world.[46] The Devil may come to destroy you, but he cannot. So, he sends a smoke screen of cares, riches and lusts to make us walk the wrong way. The thief this time is the things of this world.

God wants us to prosper and grow in every area of our lives. We are the salt of the earth and the light of the world. God wants us to be the best, the cream of the crop. The Lord is promising us success in our endeavors, not a magical transformation, like the fairy tales. The *Abundant Life* is an existence that is overflowing with a vibrant or expansionist quality.

> God is promising us success in our endeavors, not a magical transformation, like the fairy tales

Note the progression from stealing, to killing, then to destroying. First Satan comes to steal the Word from your heart, which robs us of our Faith. Therefore, guard your mind. Make sure you understand the Word and keep it (write it or read it) before you. This will ensure the Word is planted in good ground and that we are prepared to reap a harvest. Once the Word is planted the thief must wait for the first signs of life to appear.

After the seed is properly planted, the thief will attempt to kill the Word in you at the root. Temptations, sicknesses and persecutions will come to kill your joy. Consequently, choose your words carefully when you see this happening. Remember, death and life is in the power of the tongue.

Last, if the Word is allowed to take root in your heart (mind) and grow, the final thing the thief can do before you reap your harvest is to destroy the fruit. The cares of this world, the deceitfulness of riches, the pleasures of life and the lusts of the world will try to choke the effects of the Word out of you; destroying your fruit, your character, your testimony and your effectiveness as a Believer. Hence, as believers we need to watch not only our actions, but the motives behind them. Make sure we do the right thing, for the right reasons.

Note in the parable of *The Sower*, Satan is only identified in stealing the Word, not killing our joy or destroying our fruit. Why, because he has no authority to act in these areas. Believers are designed to produce fruit. It is God's best for us. We alone have the power to thwart His plans for us.

> *St. John 15:16 Ye have not chosen me, but **I have** **chosen you, and ordained you, that ye should go** **and bring forth fruit, and that your fruit should***

remain: *that whatsoever ye shall ask of the Father in my name, he may give it you.*

The scripture informs us that we have been chosen and ordained to produce fruit and our fruit will last. This is inline with the flow of the chapter, but then Jesus adds, "That whatsoever ye shall ask of the Father in my name, he may give it you." How does this line up with bearing fruit? Asking for anything in the Father's name is simply prayer.

Fruit is the produce (result) of our prayers. We plant the seed (Word of God) in our hearts, by faith. Faith is a vehicle to manifest the spiritual realities into the physical realm. Prayer is the process of planting the Word (seed) in our hearts, through faith.

Faith is a vehicle to manifest the spiritual realities into the physical realm

---

God is glorified by us bearing much fruit. In other words, The Lord is exalted when we receive the things we have asked for in prayer. Why? Think about it this way, what would be the result of the Church receiving whatever they asked for in prayer? The world would come running to the Church, seeking God. This is how our bearing much fruit brings glory to the Lord. When we glorify God in this way, it enables us to fulfill the mission of the Church.

St. Matthew 28:19 ***Go ye therefore, and teach all nations***, *baptizing them in the name of the Father, and of the Son, and of the Holy Ghost:*
St. Matthew 28:20 Teaching them to observe all things whatsoever I have commanded you: and, lo, I

am with you alway, even unto the end of the world. Amen.

The plan of God was not that we should go around witnessing and trying to convert nations to Christianity. God intended that our fruit would draw the nations to us (the Church). So when Jesus says, "Go ye therefore'. He is not telling us to move, but to apply ourselves to the task of teaching. Observe the following scriptures.

> *Jeremiah 3:17* ***At that time they shall call Jerusalem the throne of the LORD; and all the nations shall be gathered unto it,*** *to the name of the LORD, to Jerusalem: neither shall they walk any more after the imagination of their evil heart.*

> *Isaiah 2:2 And it shall come to pass* ***in the last days, that the mountain of the LORD'S house shall be established in the top of the mountains,*** *and shall be exalted above the hills;* ***and all nations shall flow unto it.***
> *Isaiah 2:3* ***And many people shall go and say, Come ye, and let us go up to the mountain of the LORD, to the house of the God*** *of Jacob;* ***and he will teach us of his ways,*** *and we will walk in his paths: for out of Zion shall go forth the law, and the word of the LORD from Jerusalem.*

Clearly, in these Old Testament prophecies God is telling us that the nations will come to us, not we to them. Why will the nations come to us? The answer is simple. Success attracts people like a magnet. Jesus has commissioned us to instruct the nations and to baptize them. In other words, He wants us to make them disciples. When we do this, we expand the Kingdom of God, via the Church. We must understand. Jesus is not commissioning us to teach the religion of Christianity. He is telling us to teach the principles of the Kingdom, meaning how to live the Abundant Life.

Jesus clearly stated that He came to give us (the world) abundant life. Christ's mission and the message of the Bible is restoration. Jesus is the second Adam restoring what we lost in the first. The first Adam was neither a Jew nor a Christian. He was a child of God. Both Adam and Eve had two things in the beginning. They had a relationship with God and dominion over the whole earth.

Why do you think God gives us Abundant Life? In this world, there is unimaginable suffering, people are in despair. It is our nature to look for help outside of ourselves. We search for God. Jesus gives us Abundant Life because we are the manifestation of the invisible God. We are the living, tangible proof that God exists. We are meant to be the undeniable, inexplicable love of God in action. This is the true call of the Church. The continual demonstration of our faith is what draws people into the Kingdom.

We are proof of God. If we live our lives according to this truth, we will not have to ask, "What would Jesus do." Abundant Life is much more than a gift from God. It is His mandate for us.

We are the tangible proof of God

We cannot allow the thief to steal, kill and destroy any longer. We must from this day forward live abundantly, victorious through the power of God.

Remember the story of the old carpenter who was ready to retire. He told his employer of his plan to leave and his boss was sad to see him go. The employer asked the carpenter to build just one more house. He reluctantly agreed. The carpenter did sloppy work and used inferior materials, just to finish as quickly as possible.

After the carpenter finished, the employer came to inspect the house. Then he handed the keys to the carpenter. Congratulations, said the employer. The house is yours. This is my retirement gift to you. The carpenter was in shock. If he had only known he was building his own house, he would not have cut corners.

Learn the lesson of the carpenter. Understand that we are building together with God. The construction process is our lives. The good building materials are love, joy, peace, longsuffering and so on. The question is. How will we build? Know that in the end, we will have to live with whatever we have built. The apostle Paul put it this way.

> *1 Corinthians 3:9 **For we are labourers together with God**: ye are God's husbandry, ye are God's building.*
> *1 Corinthians 3:10 According to the grace of God which is given unto me, as a wise masterbuilder, I have laid the foundation, and another buildeth thereon. **But let every man take heed how he buildeth thereupon.***
> *1 Corinthians 3:11 For other foundation can no man lay than that is laid, which is Jesus Christ.*
> *1 Corinthians 3:12 Now if any man build upon this foundation gold, silver, precious stones, wood, hay, stubble;*
> *1 Corinthians 3:13 **Every man's work shall be made manifest**: for the day shall declare it, because it shall be revealed by fire; and the fire shall try every man's work of what sort it is.*

1 Corinthians 3:14 **If any man's work abide which he hath built thereupon, he shall receive a reward.**

You are the carpenter! This is why Paul says of us that we are, "Workman that need not to be ashamed and who correctly handle the Word of Truth."[47]

Chapter 7

Effective Prayer

Ask, and it shall be given you; seek, and ye shall find; knock, and it shall be opened unto you: For every one that asketh receiveth; and he that seeketh findeth; and to him that knocketh it shall be opened.

St. Matthew 7:7-8

There has been much written on the subject of how to pray effectively. Even so, what is an effective prayer? Any prayer which produces the desired request or object is an effective prayer. In short, answered prayer is effective prayer.

There are very few rules or forms to praying, but there are some principles to getting answered prayer. I will not go into them, since there are plenty of books on the subject.

- Fervent (James 5:16)
- Persistent (St. Luke 18:3-8)
- In Faith (James 1:6-7)
- Sincere (St. Matthew 6:5-8)

If we look at the story of the woman with the issue of blood, I believe we will find yet another important principle of effective prayer.

> *St. Mark 5:25 And a **certain woman, which had an issue of blood twelve years,***
> *St. Mark 5:26 And had suffered many things of many physicians, and had spent all that she had, and was nothing bettered, but rather grew worse,*
> *St. Mark 5:27 **When she had heard of Jesus, came in the press behind, and touched his garment.***
> *St. Mark 5:28 For **she said, If I may touch but his clothes, I shall be whole.***
> *St. Mark 5:29 **And straightway the fountain of her blood was dried up**; and she felt in her body that she was healed of that plague.*
> *St. Mark 5:30 **And Jesus, immediately knowing in himself that virtue had gone out of him,** turned him about in the press, and **said, Who touched my clothes?***
> *St. Mark 5:31 And his disciples said unto him, Thou seest the multitude thronging thee, and sayest thou, Who touched me?*
> *St. Mark 5:32 And he looked round about to see her that had done this thing.*
> *St. Mark 5:33 But the woman fearing and trembling, knowing what was done in her, came and fell down before him, and told him all the truth.*
> *St. Mark 5:34 And he said unto her, Daughter, thy faith hath made thee whole; go in peace, and be whole of thy plague.*

A certain woman suffered many things from many physicians for twelve long years and at the end of all this, she got worse. However, when things apparently could not get any worse and all money and hope were gone. God steps on the scene.

> *Isaiah 42:8* **I am the LORD***: that is my name:* **and my glory will I not give to another**, *neither my praise to graven images.*

God does not need the glory or the credit because He has a super ego. The Lord wants all the glory, so that when the next storm comes your way, you will know where to run and in whom to put your trust. God will allow you to go through, so that your faith will endure and you will become stable, in good times and bad.

How long have you been suffering? Have you tried everything and it failed, including prayer. Sometimes God allows us to go through until we have exhausted every other alternate for help. That is not always the case, but sometimes it is. In these times, nothing and no one else can get the credit (glory) but God.

The first question we should ask is why did the woman believe that touching the hem of Jesus' garment would cause her to be healed? Where did she get such a notion? According to the book of St. Mark, this woman was not the only person who thought this way.

> *St. Mark 6:56 And* **wherever he [Jesus] went—into villages, towns or countryside—** *they placed the sick in the market-places.* **They begged him to let them touch even the edge of his cloak,** *and all who touched him were healed.*

The edge of the cloak or hem of the garment actually refers to the fringes of the prayer shawls (Tallits) that the Jews wore. A *tallit* is worn during the morning prayers

(Shacharit) on weekdays, the Sabbath and Holy days. The tallit has special twined and knotted fringes known as *tzitzit* attached to its four corners. The tallit can be made of any material except a mixture of wool and linen (shatnez) interwoven, which are strictly prohibited by the Torah.

The fringe or tassel in ancient times was considered an extension of the owner and more specifically of the owner's rank and authority. It also was a way to identify those of nobility.

Remember, Jesus warned about the Pharisees, who love to be seen of men and honored. This is why they made their phylacteries wide and the tassels on their garments long (St. Matthew 23:1-12), so their rank or status could be clearly seen by everybody. Kind of like today, with ministers wearing Catholic attire and using Catholic titles just to look more important, but I digress.

What happens when you touch or grab hold of the tassels? Requests accompanied by grasping the fringes of the one from whom you wanted something could not be refused. Therefore, this was not an act of humility on the woman's part. It was not because she wanted to make Jesus ritually unclean. Touching Christ's garment while it was on his body, was just like touching him, He would in effective become unclean from her touch.

This woman risked all and pressed her way through the crowd in her weakened and unclean condition, to issue a request that could not be refused. She knew Christ could heal her, but she needed to put Him in a position where He could not refuse her. There was no special anointing in the garments of Jesus. We lost the true implication behind the woman's action, because time has obscured the original meaning of touching the fringe of the garment.

Today Jesus is not physically walking around so what do we do? We must understand the symbolic meaning behind the story. The tassels or fringes represent the Word of God.

> *Numbers 15:38* **Speak unto the children of Israel, and bid them that they make them fringes in the borders of their garments throughout their generations,** *and that they put upon the fringe of the borders a ribband of blue:*
> *Numbers 15:39* **And it shall be unto you for a fringe, that ye may look upon it, and remember all the commandments of the LORD, and do them;** *and that ye seek not after your own heart and your own eyes, after which ye use to go a whoring:*

This is the reason that knotting the fringes has evolved. The twists and knots total 613, to coincide with the number of commands in the Jewish law. The tassels on the prayer shawl represent the commandments of God, in other words, they symbolize God's Word.

Therefore, whenever you need something, you must press through the crowd (circumstances, emotions or people). The crowd is anything that stands between you and the Lord. Reach out a grab a hold of the hem of Christ's garment. The hem or tassel represents His Word. Understand that whenever you grab hold of the Word for a specific thing, God cannot refuse your request. For example, if you need healing, find a scripture that promises you healing and do not let go of it until you get healed. God cannot refuse this type of prayer.

We know at the name of Jesus every knee must bow. However, the Bible declares that God will honor His Word above His name. This means that He places performing

His Word above receiving your worship and praise. God is not a king like other kings. When you come before a king, you must present a gift and appease him before you can ever make a request. The king could deny your request and you would walk away empty handed.

God is more interested in blessing you, than having you bless Him. The Word declares that we should come boldly before the throne of Grace. You never come before an earthly king boldly. The apostle John puts it this way.

> *1 John 5:14* **This is the confidence we have in approaching God**: *that if we ask anything according to his will, he hears us.*
> *1 John 5:15 And if we know that he hears us—whatever we ask—***we know that we have what we asked of him.**

Get what you need from God. Come boldly before His throne in prayer, grab hold of His Word and declare it until you get what you need. This is one of the most important principles of effective prayer and abundant life.

Touch the hem of His garment

There has been a recent move within the Church to incorporate Jewish prayer shawls (Tallits) into Christianity. As we saw with the woman with the issue of blood, there was no special anointing in the shawl itself. It does not absorb the prayers and anointing of the wearer. Paul addressed this issue of having Gentiles follow Jewish customs in the book of Galatians.

The Message Bible

> *Galatians 6:15* **Can't you see the central issue in all this? It is not what you and I do**—*submit to*

*circumcision, reject circumcision. **It is what God is doing**, and he is creating something totally new, a free life!*
*Galatians 6:16 **All who walk by this standard are the true Israel of God**—his chosen people.*

The things that pertain to the Old Testament were just examples and shadows of what were to come through Christ. Jesus came and gave us a better covenant based on better promises, why would we need to go back and get anything from the old? Whom the Son sets free is free indeed.

Do not allow others to exploit you. The anointing, healings and blessings of God cannot be bought. They are given freely and directly by God. No man or item is needed to bless you, because God has already done it through Christ Jesus and His Word. Simply walk in His promises.

Chapter 8

The Principle of Agreement

Again I say unto you, that if two of you shall agree on earth as touching any thing that they shall ask, it shall be done for them of my Father which is in heaven.

St. Matthew 18:19

We touched on the principle of agreement earlier in chapter one. Now we will look at it in a little more depth. Reciprocity will reproduce your thoughts into physical form. It does not distinguish good from evil. The law is designed to produce whatever you desire. This is the reason the apostle Paul admonishes us to focus our thoughts on things that are honest, true, pure, lovely or of a good report (Philippians 4:8).

We all have random thoughts. Paul is not referring to them. He is talking about the things we meditate on or think deeply about, the things that become part of our psyche. Fortunately, thoughts alone do not manifest things into reality. That would have catastrophic results. Our words must coincide with our thoughts. Here is where the principle of agreement comes into play.

The Law of Agreement does not just apply to people, but it is applicable to our faith. So, reciprocity will reproduce your thoughts into a physical form, but only when there is agreement between the mental, verbal and physical processes. Why then does Paul in the book of Philippians stress what we mentally think about?

> *St. Matthew 12:34 O generation of vipers, how can ye, being evil, speak good things?* ***for out of the abundance of the heart the mouth speaketh.***

The mouth speaks what is in the heart (mind), so if we guard our thoughts, our lips will cause us no harm. What are words really? Words are the embodiment of our thoughts, used to communicate with others. Since reciprocity does not distinguish positive from negative, we need to guard our minds and our tongues.

Faith and fear are built upon identical principles. They are simply at opposite ends of the spectrum.

Faith = Belief (thoughts) + Words + Actions
Fear = Belief (thoughts) + Words + Actions

Two is the minimum number necessary for agreement, but there are three parts to faith. Therefore, if you absolutely need to manifest something, you should get the agreement of all three.

> *Ecclesiastes 4:12 And **if one prevail against him, two shall withstand him; and a threefold cord is not quickly broken.***

Solomon lays out the principle of agreement in the book of Ecclesiastes. This principle gives us the formula for success against any obstacle, spiritual or physical. Why do we need a procedure? The Bible clearly says, "If God be for us who can be against us."[48] The Lord is always on our side, but we still must have faith, because without it, we cannot please God.[49]

Faith	1. **Belief**
	2. **Words**
	3. **Actions**

Faith has three components, belief, words and actions. It has the threefold principle of agreement built into it. Solomon's formula presumes that there is someone or something against you. Sometimes it is people, other times there are obstacles in your way and on occasion, the odds are just not in your favor. Whatever it is utilize the formula, which is all the components of faith and you cannot lose.

Opposition	vs	1 component	=	Unpredictable results
Opposition	vs	2 components	=	Will withstand or stop
Opposition	vs	3 components	=	Will subdue completely

As they say, "Two out of three ain't bad." But, clearly, three is far superior to two. Three means absolute and total victory over any opposition and that is something we all want. The question becomes does Solomon's advice also apply to our faith?

In order to answer this question, there is a second piece of the Law of Agreement in the book of James, which I think we should look at.

*James 1:6 **But let him ask in faith, nothing
wavering.** For he that wavereth is like a wave of the
sea driven with the wind and tossed.
James 1:7 **For let not that man think that he shall
receive any thing of the Lord.**
James 1:8 A double minded man is unstable in all
his ways.*

If we combine St. Matthew 18:19 with James 1:6-8, we see
the whole principle and we get a slightly different view.

The Law of Agreement
*If two of you shall agree on earth as touching any
thing that they shall ask, it shall be done for them of
my Father which is in heaven. But let them ask in
faith, nothing wavering. For those that wavereth
are like a wave of the sea driven with the wind and
tossed. For let not them think that they shall
receive any thing of the Lord. A double minded
person is unstable in all their ways.*

According to the Law of Agreement, two out of three is
bad. Why? There must be harmony between what you
think, speak and do, in order for faith to work. If there is
disagreement, your faith will fail to produce.

Anyone who has been in Church for any amount of time is
familiar with the *Wall of Jericho* story in the Bible. Joshua
led the Israelites to march around the wall of Jericho, one
time for six days. However, on the seventh day they
marched around the wall seven times, shouted and the wall
fell flat.

This transpired in Joshua chapter six, but here is the
backdrop to the story. In chapter one Moses died. This had
a big negative impact of Israel. Joshua becomes the new

and yet unproven leader, another negative. Joshua then sends two spies to check out Jericho. They are almost caught, but Rahab the prostitute helps them escape. The fact that she puts her life at risk to save the two spies is a much needed positive sign. Next, the Ark passes before the children of Israel in the Jordan River and the waters are dried up. This miracle is a great confidence builder under Joshua's leadership. Once Israel crosses over the Jordan into enemy territory, Joshua has all the men circumcised. Circumcision before a war to say the least is probably not a good move logically speaking. But, in the opponent's backyard, it is insanity. Last of all they observed Passover. This observance would cause Israel to remember their mighty deliverance by the hand of God. This is by far one of the biggest pluses for a group about to go to war.

*Joshua 6:10 And **Joshua had commanded the people, saying, Ye shall not shout, nor make any noise with your voice, neither shall any word proceed out of your mouth, until the day I bid you shout**; then shall ye shout.*

Joshua did not allow anyone to speak for seven days. Why? From a human perspective, the only thing that could come out of the Israelites mouths was fear. No one in Israel had ever faced war before, not even Joshua. Their first military campaign was to take Jericho. This was the most important city and the strongest fortress in all the land of Canaan.

If they were allowed to open their mouths and express what they saw and felt, they probably would have negatively used the power of agreement and caused their own downfall. Joshua wisely forbade Israel to speak. The last thing they heard before going to battle was the power of God during Passover, this built up their belief system. As they marched around the wall, they showed that their actions were in agreement with their beliefs.

Joshua chose to go with two out of three components of agreement (faith). But more importantly he stopped Israel from wavering with their words and being in disagreement.

Remember, Joshua was one of the original twelve spies whom Moses sent into the land earlier. Ten of them gave a negative (evil) report and caused forty years of wandering through the wilderness. This setback undoubtedly played through his mind countless times and he was not about to repeat it.

No weapon, circumstance or problem can overcome you, unless you agree to it. Jesus said, "If two of you shall agree on earth as touching any thing that they shall ask, it shall be done for them of my Father which is in heaven."[50] Normally, we restrict this principle to prayer, because of the word "ask". But, when you replace the term with its synonyms (speak, require or expect), the restriction drops. Now you begin to get the full flavor of the scripture and the power of unity. Agreement works for both good and evil. This is the point of the *Tower of Babel*.

> *Genesis 11:6 And **the LORD said, Behold, the people is one**, and they have all one language; and this they begin to do: **and now nothing will be restrained from them, which they have imagined to do**.*

The principle and power of agreement are not limited to finding a prayer partner. Certainly, it applies to our prayer life, but it also applies to our endeavors, our circumstances and every other area of our life.

No weapon, circumstance or problem can overcome you, unless you agree to it

Fortunately, the words of others cannot affect us, unless we agree with them. In fact, nothing can overcome us, unless we first give it our consent. Whenever we believe, repeat or act in accordance to what we see or hear, we form an agreement.

For example, if the doctor tells you that you have high blood pressure and you start telling people what the doctor said. That is an agreement. I am not advocating that you live in denial. No, instead live in faith. Try this, change your diet, take your medicine, exercise regularly and say, "I walk in divine health; my blood pressure is 110 over 70." Start monitoring your pressure, write down the readings and when it starts to get close to normal have your doctor re-evaluate it.

After the doctor takes you off your blood pressure lowering medication, do not go back to your old habits. A lot of Christians do and when their pressure is back up, guess who gets the blame, the Devil. Keep eating right, exercising and monitoring your pressure. This is true agreement. **This is faith in its proper perspective.**

You can declare all day long that you walk in divine health, but if you refuse to exercise and eat properly, what effect will your words have? If you do not have an agreement between what you believe, speak and do, the Bible calls you a wavering person. The book of James puts in this way "Let not that man think that he shall receive any thing of the Lord."[51] My advice is when in doubt, close your mouth.

Proverbs 21:2 He who guards his mouth and his
tongue keeps himself from calamity.

Parents used to say, "If you don't have anything good to say, don't say anything." Sometimes our faith is low. In those times, we can take a lesson from Joshua and just shut up for awhile. We must understand that if we want the walls to fall in our lives, then we must speak in accordance to God's Word or not at all. We need to remain silent, concerning everything else no matter how valid or real is seems.

When in doubt, close your mouth

Why do our thoughts, words and actions generate what we believe? As I stated earlier, God is not a benevolent entity who sits in heaven answering our prayers individually. That would be an extremely inefficient method to meet the needs of humanity. So, God created the universe and everything in it to conform to the Law of Reciprocity. It is the primary Law of this world.

The Law of Attraction is a metaphysical belief that states, positive and negative thinking brings about positive and negative physical results, respectively. According to the Law, the phrase "I need more money" allows the person to continue to "need more money." If the person wants to change this, they would focus their thoughts on the goal (having more money) rather than the problem (needing more money). This might take the form of phrases, such as "I will make more money" or "I will find a job that pays very well."

The Law of Attraction has been criticized for its lack of refutability and testability. Critics have asserted that the evidence provided is usually anecdotal and because of the

100

subjective nature of any results, they are prone to bias. For this reason, we will take a different approach to viewing the Law of Attraction, namely science.

The electric charges coursing through the human brain are measurable by using an electroencephalogram. Electroencephalography (EEG) is the recording of electrical activity along the scalp produced by the firing of neurons within the brain. Humans generate an electromagnetic energy field. As a result of this, the body could act as an aerial that has the potential for simultaneous transmission and reception of energy with its environment. Humanity has an inherent connection with its environment, the basis of which is human consciousness itself, something which is now quantifiable, at least on a theoretical basis.[52]

What do we know about electromagnetism? It is one of the four fundamental interactions of nature. Electromagnetism is responsible for practically all the phenomena encountered in daily life, except for gravity.

We saw earlier in chapter two that Faith is proportional and operates according to Ohm's Law of electricity. That explains how we transmit positive or negative results when we are praying for others, but how do we attract blessings to ourselves?

We attract things to us through magnetism. An electromagnet is a type of magnet whose magnetic field is produced by the flow of electric current (faith). A straight current-carrying wire, for instance, produces a magnetic field that points neither towards nor away from the wire, but encircles it instead. The strength of magnetic field generated is proportional to the amount of current (faith or fear).

So when you transmit hateful thoughts, words or actions, you automatically draw to yourself, anything that is attracted to hate, such as violence, hostility, anger, bitterness, just to name a few. Likewise, when you transmit loving thoughts, words or actions, you inevitably draw things that are attracted to love, such as tenderness, benevolence, devotion, enthusiasm, admiration and the like.

It is because of the Law of Attraction that Jesus admonishes us to always to love. This includes those who we feel or know do not deserve it.

> *St. Matthew 5:44 But **I say unto you, Love your enemies, bless them** that curse you, **do good to them** that hate you, **and pray for them** which despitefully use you, and persecute you;*

According to the Principles of Electromagnetism (The Laws of Faith and Attraction) we receive in direct proportion to our belief, because the same intensity we transmit encircles us with a magnetic field that draws equally back to us. This scientific principle relates to the natural law and correlates perfectly to the spiritual law given in the Bible.

You do not have to understand the science behind the concept. What is important is that it works for you. Test it for yourself and see.

Chapter 9

Stewardship

And the Lord said, Who then is that faithful and wise steward, whom his lord shall make ruler over his household, to give them their portion of meat in due season?

St. Luke 12:42

A steward is someone typically employed in a large household or estate to manage domestic concerns (e.g. as the supervision of servants, collection of rents, and keeping of accounts). Today, we would call that person a manager.

Are all believers considered stewards of God? Is this a biblical view? As we know Jesus always taught spiritual truths in parable form. Observe what the scriptures have to say about it.

<u>KJV</u>
St. Luke 19:11 And as they heard these things, he added and spake a parable, because he was nigh to Jerusalem, and because they thought that the kingdom of God should immediately appear.

St. Luke 19:12 He said therefore, A certain nobleman went into a far country to receive for himself a kingdom, and to return.
St. Luke 19:13 And he called his ten servants, and delivered them ten pounds, and said unto them, **Occupy till I come.**

NIV

St. Luke 19:13 So he called ten of his servants and gave them ten minas. **'Put this money to work,' he said, 'until I come back.'**

Jesus is the nobleman that has gone into a far country to receive a Kingdom for Himself and believers are His servants. I showed St. Luke 19:13 in the New International Version, to flush out the true meaning of what it means to occupy in the KJV. Why are ten servants given ten pounds?

Ten is the number of man's responsibility before God or testing. There are Ten Commandments given to Israel, as their duty before the Lord (Exodus 20:1-17). Ten is the number of testing. The Church in Smyrna was tested by tribulation for ten days (Revelation 2:10). Daniel had the prince of the eunuchs wait ten days before deciding their dietary provisions (Daniel 1:12).[53]

Our responsibility or test while Christ is away from us is to occupy until He returns. The NIV puts it this way, "Put this money to work ... until I come back." What money? I can almost hear some saying like Job, "Naked came I out of my mother's womb and naked will I return."[54] This is certainly true, but what about the time between birth and death?

Deuteronomy 8:17 And thou say in thine heart, My power and the might of mine hand hath gotten me this wealth.
Deuteronomy 8:18 ***But thou shalt remember the LORD thy God: for it is he that giveth thee power to get wealth,*** *that he may establish his covenant which he sware unto thy fathers, as it is this day.*

Ecclesiastes 5:19 ***Every man also to whom God hath given riches and wealth,*** *and hath given him power to eat thereof, and to take his portion, and to rejoice in his labour;* ***this is the gift of God.***

So, every dollar we earn is considered a gift from God, even though we worked for it. The money Jesus instructs us to put to work until He returns is what we earn throughout our lifetime. Christ has made us stewards over the money we make. Which is probably more than we imagined?

Statistics reveal that in the U.S. over an adult's working life, they will earn on average:[55]

High school graduates	$1.2 million
Bachelor's degree	$2.1 million
Master's degree	$2.5 million
Doctoral degrees	$3.4 million
Professional degrees	$4.4 million

That is quite a sum to be entrusted with. There are two vital elements every person needs in order to be considered a good steward.

1. **Trustworthy** - reliable, responsible, solid, steady, sure, tried-and-true, trustable, dependable, faithful

2. **Proficient** - accomplished, adept, good, great, masterful, skillful, versed

We need to be both trustworthy and proficient over the finances God has given us.

Is Jesus really talking about money in the parable or could He be referring to our physical and mental talents? St. Luke 16:1-15 which is better known as the parable of the "Unjust Steward," gives us some more insight on the subject.

> *St. Luke 16:8 And the lord commended the unjust steward, because he had done wisely: **for the children of this world are in their generation wiser than the children of light.***
> *St. Luke 16:9 And I say unto you, **Make to yourselves friends of the mammon of unrighteousness; that, when ye fail, they may receive you into everlasting habitations.***
> *St. Luke 16:10 He that is faithful in that which is least is faithful also in much: and he that is unjust in the least is unjust also in much.*
> *St. Luke 16:11 **If therefore ye have not been faithful in the unrighteous mammon, who will commit to your trust the true riches?***
> *St. Luke 16:12 And if ye have not been faithful in that which is another man's, who shall give you that which is your own?*

Christ is definitely talking about money. In this parable, Jesus contrasts an untrustworthy steward of a certain rich man (also called lord) to Christians. If this comparison was not odd enough, He goes on to tell us to make friends with money to gain eternal dwellings.

The unjust steward was not trustworthy, but when he was about to lose his stewardship, he demonstrated that he was very proficient. The steward's lord (the land owner) commended his skillfulness not his reliability. Jesus' commentary on the parable is that the children of this world (sinners) are wiser in their dealings with money than the children of light (believers). After He deals with proficiency, He goes on to emphasize our faithfulness (trustworthiness) in regard to money. The intent of Jesus' words is definitely obscure.

KJV

St. Luke 16: 9 ***And I say unto you, Make to yourselves friends of the mammon of unrighteousness****; that, when ye fail, they may receive you into everlasting habitations.*

NIV

St. Luke 16:9 ***I tell you, use worldly wealth to gain friends for yourselves, so that when it is gone****, you will be welcomed into eternal dwellings.*

Neither the King James Version nor the New International Version sheds much light on what Jesus is trying to tell us. The unjust steward found out that his job was gone. He quickly accessed his situation and determined what to do. The steward's lord commended his shrewdness. Jesus appraises the parable and declares that the world is wiser in their financial affairs than the Church.

Since this is Jesus' evaluation of believers, we will assume this is a fact. So, we need to see why this is true? Understand that Christ is speaking in generalities. The world understands the system (economic realities) and will make it work for them. They are proficient (wise). The Church focuses almost exclusively on being faithful (trustworthy). Jesus is trying to show us that we need to be both trustworthy and proficient with money.

"Money is neither bad nor good. Like water or fire, money is powerful, but neutral. Your body needs water to live, but water can also drown you. Fire can keep you warm, but it can also burn you. The same goes for money. It is often used for good (feeding your family, protecting others), but it can also be used for evil (as a means of control or an object of unhealthy obsession)."[56]

Why does Jesus tell us to make friends with money? When Christ tells us to make friends with money, He is telling us to become acquainted or intimate with it. The Message Bible hits the nail on the head, probably because it is not a literal translation.

Message Bible

St. Luke 16: 8-9 Now here's a surprise: The master praised the crooked manager! And why? Because he knew how to look after himself. Streetwise people are smarter in this regard than law-abiding citizens. They are on constant alert, looking for angles, surviving by their wits. I want you to be smart in the same way—but for what is right—using every adversity to stimulate you to be creative for survival, to concentrate your attention on the bare essentials, so you'll live, really live, and not complacently just get by on good behavior.

As I said earlier, Jesus is telling us to be trustworthy and proficient with money, but how does that relate to eternal life? The money God has entrusted to us is not to be used solely for our benefit, but to further the Kingdom of God. This is how becoming acquainted with finances will make us welcomed into everlasting habitations. When we are wise over the resources that God has given us, we are well pleasing to Him.

Remember earlier in the chapter on Abundant Life we saw that Israel was told to enlarge the place of their tent. God instructed them to make their dwelling place bigger, by spreading out to the left and the right. The prophet Isaiah foretold of Christ's Kingdom saying, "The increase of his government and peace there will be no end."[57]   God expects us to use our monies to expand His Kingdom. The Kingdom of God is not increased simply through adding converts.   Believers must become trustworthy and proficient with their finances, because in this world, money is power.

The Kingdom of God is always associated with power. If Christians are poor, our influence is only spiritual. However, if we are financially stable, our influence will be increased dramatically. As we stated earlier in the book, "People are naturally drawn to success."

We started out this chapter with two questions. Are all believers considered stewards of God and is this a biblical view?   The answer is a resounding, "Yes" to both questions. The only question left is when Christ returns will He judge you to be a good steward of His resources?

Let me digress for a moment on the subject of tithes and offerings. They are not our seeds, but our produce (I will explain this more in the next chapter) we need to clearly see the blessings of God come from obedience to His Word, not sacrificial offerings.

*Deuteronomy 28:1 And it shall come to pass, **if thou shalt hearken diligently unto the voice of the LORD thy God, to observe and to do all his***

commandments which I command thee this day,
that the LORD thy God will set thee on high above
all nations of the earth:

When Israel paid their tithes they were not blessed because of the amount. They were blessed because of their obedience to God's command to tithe. It was their obedience that determined how blessed they were, not their sacrifice. In other words, God enriches us due to our obedience. He is not blessing our tithes. If He increases the offerings that we give to Him, what good would that do us? It is the seed in our pockets or possession that require God's favor, not the money we put in the offering plate.

The point of all this is to get clarity. By all means continue to pay your tithes and offerings to your particular Church. However, do not get bamboozled by clergy members, who manipulate scriptures to empty your pockets.

> The blessings of God come from obedience to His Word, not sacrificial offerings

God does not. I repeat does not ask you for an offering in order to bless you. The Word declares that if you walk in obedience to His written Word, then you are already blessed. Simply access His promises through faith.

God also requires that we obey His Spirit and here is where it gets tricky. The little voice inside you is how God speaks to you, primarily. Pastors, prophets and the like should only confirm what the Spirit tells you on the inside or the Spirit will confirm what they tell you. Do not take anyone solely at their word without confirmation from the Spirit of God, no matter how anointed they happen to be. I suspect that I may be excommunicated from the Church due to this, but it is true anyhow.

The days of taking a prophet's words without confirmation ended on the day of Pentecost. That was Old Testament procedure.

> *1 John 2:26* ***These things have I written unto you concerning them that seduce you.***
> *1 John 2:27* But ***the anointing which ye have received of him abideth in you, and ye need not that any man teach you: but as the same anointing teacheth you of all things****, and is truth, and is no lie, and even as it hath taught you, ye shall abide in him.*

Some do these things out of ignorance. Some due to tradition and others are no more than holy hustlers, preying on the believer's willingness to please God. Arm yourself with the Word of God. This is why the scriptures urge us to rightly divide the Truth.[58]

We must understand that we do not give God our seeds, but it is the Lord who gives us the seeds.

> *2 Corinthians 9:10* ***Now he [God] who supplies seed to the sower*** *and bread for food will also supply and increase your store of seed and will enlarge the harvest of your righteousness.*

> *Deuteronomy 14:22* ***Thou shalt truly tithe all the increase of thy seed****, that the field bringeth forth year by year.*

If God does not require our seeds, then how can the Church be fertile ground to plant? It cannot. We are supposed to come to the Church and present our produce (fruit) as an offering of thanksgiving for how God has increased or multiplied our seeds.

Seed faith offerings as they are called, are a sham. You cannot invest money into the Kingdom of God. Why? Money is a tangible medium of exchange. The Kingdom is spiritual. Thus, it cannot be invested into through a physical mode. In finances, an investment is putting money into something with the expectation of gain. We cannot pay God to be blessed.

> *Acts 8:18 And **when Simon saw that through laying on of the apostles' hands the Holy Ghost was given, he offered them money,***
> *Acts 8:19 Saying, Give me also this power, that on whomsoever I lay hands, he may receive the Holy Ghost.*
> *Acts 8:20 **But Peter said unto him, Thy money perish with thee, because thou hast thought that the gift of God may be purchased with money.***

Spiritual things cannot be obtained by money. I do not care if you change the words from "purchasing" to "planting", it is impossible.

Understand that your seed is something that you receive benefits from personally and directly. When you give to the Church, the Church does not send you money to pay your bills. The money you give pays the Church's bills. I can almost hear someone saying that God blesses us in more ways than financially. What about our health?

Seeds like all things in this world operate by laws. A seed can only reproduce after its kind. Meaning an apple seed can only produce apples. It does not matter that you desperately need oranges, if you plant apple seeds, apples are what you get. Therefore, you cannot plant money as your seed and reap health, protection, long life or anything else but increased materials and wealth. It is the law of the seed.

Things like health, protection and long life come through our obedience to God's Word, not our financial seeds. Do not be duped by spiritual sounding arguments. God does not initiate $500.00 lines with your blessings dangling like a carrot in front of you. That is extortion, plain and simple.

For example, if you want health, God's Word outlines dietary restrictions for His people. The original diet for humans was vegetarian, but after sin entered meat was introduced (highlighting the need for sacrifices). Even after meat was allowed, there were certain restrictions as to which meats could be eaten. After Christ's first Advent, all restrictions were removed, because He was the true sacrifice. However, that does not mean we should not use common sense in choosing our foods. Note that along with this dietary progression, there was a corresponding decline in the lifespan of humans.

We should also note the fact that after meat was introduced, so was the concept of fasting. The body needs a break from constant meat eating. In addition, humans need regular exercise, throughout the biblical times humans walked everywhere. Life itself was an aerobic workout. All of these things are the seeds to reaping good health. Simply remember that the body is a temple for the Holy Spirit. That being the case, we would do well to take good care of it. These are the seeds to good health, not offerings.

St. Matthew 10:16 Behold, I send you forth as sheep in the midst of wolves: **be ye therefore wise as serpents, and harmless as doves.**

Solomon said wisdom is the most important thing to get, with it, we will know how to manage everything in life. Without it how can we possibly be good stewards?

Chapter 10

The Place of Wealth

Praise ye the LORD. Blessed is the man that feareth the LORD, that delighteth greatly in his commandments.
His seed shall be mighty upon earth: the generation of the upright shall be blessed.
Wealth and riches shall be in his house: and his righteousness endureth for ever.

Psalms 112:1-3

There has historically been a pattern in the life of the Christian Church, wherein members of the body of Christ separated themselves to be consecrated to a more contemplative lifestyle, or decided to live in voluntary poverty in order to meet the needs of the world.

Does the Bible consider wealth to be against holiness? This is a valid question since the Bible is a spiritual book and we are talking about material wealth.

*Deuteronomy 8:18 But thou shalt remember the LORD thy God: **for it is he that giveth thee power to get wealth, that he may establish his covenant which he sware unto thy fathers**, as it is this day.*

Normally, we stop at God giving us the power to get wealth, but it says He does this in order to establish His covenant with Israel. What does the covenant have to do with wealth?

> *Deuteronomy 28:2* **And all these blessings shall come on thee, and overtake thee, if thou shalt hearken unto the voice of the LORD thy God.**

> *Deuteronomy 28:11* **And the LORD shall make thee plenteous in goods** *[material things], in the fruit of thy body [labor force],* **and in the fruit of thy cattle** *[wealth],* **and in the fruit of thy ground** *[food], in the land which the LORD sware unto thy fathers to give thee.*

> *Deuteronomy 28:12* **The LORD shall open unto thee his good treasure,** *the heaven to give the rain unto thy land in his season,* **and to bless all the work of thine hand: and thou shalt lend unto many nations, and thou shalt not borrow.**

Included in the covenant between God and Israel were blessings of wealth, for obedience to the Law. This was not an added benefit of the covenant. It was in God's mind from the beginning. Why? No one can definitely answer for God, but I believe there is a twofold reason. The first is because humans are not purely spiritual beings, but we are also terrestrial. Therefore, we have both spiritual and physical requirements that need to be fulfilled. Second wealth served as a magnet to draw other nations to Israel and ultimately to the God of Israel.

It is impossible to live the *Abundant Life* on strictly a spiritual plane. The life Jesus promised us encompasses every area, spiritual, mental and physical.

"It is terribly important that you bury, once and for all, the myth that money is bad or unimportant. Money is not bad. As the Bible says, "love of money is the cause of evil." Money is important to anyone living in a civilized society and to argue that it's not important is absurd. Let us be realistic enough to face the facts of life and demand from life the best that it can give. Nothing will take the place of money in the area in which money works."[59]

Money is probably the number one reason given for not living to our fullest? God includes it in His blessing plan for us. Deuteronomy 8:18 makes it clear that God gives us the power or ability to get wealth. So how do we obtain wealth?

Henry Ford was quoted as saying, "If he lost his billion-dollar fortune, that he would have it back in less than five years."[60] How? This is because he understood the process of building wealth. We have all heard of athletes, entertainers and lottery winners who have lost untold millions and never got it back. Why, because they did not understand how to build wealth, they just had fortunate circumstances.

Just because a minister lays hands on you and commands poverty to leave. This alone will not make you wealthy. We can declare that money comes all day long, place our bills on the altar, but that alone does not make it so. We need knowledge and understanding of how to obtain wealth. Declaring the Word of God, is only part of the part of the process. The words of Hosea ring true, "My people are destroyed for lack of knowledge."

If money is your hope for independence, you will never have it. The only real security that a man will have in this world is a reserve of knowledge, experience, and ability.

- Henry Ford -

We are all familiar with the phrase, "Knowledge is power," but what does it really mean? **Knowledge** - the fact or condition of knowing something with familiarity gained through experience or association; it is the range of one's information or understanding; in other words, knowledge comes from learning or understanding something.

Wisdom, on the other hand, is slightly different from knowledge. **Wisdom** - ability to discern inner qualities and relationships; wisdom is characterized by discernment (detect with the senses), insight (seeing past the facts), perception (awareness).

Knowledge alone will not guarantee wealth, but when it is coupled with wisdom it does. Knowledge will tell you how to do something, but wisdom will give you the what, when and the where. This is paramount because we know that in life timing is everything.

So, how do we get the proper knowledge and wisdom we need in the life? Knowledge comes through applying ourselves. There is no shortcut to knowledge. True wisdom, on the other hand, comes directly from God. God will do His part, but we must do ours.

*2 Timothy 1:7 **For God hath** not **given us** the spirit of fear; but of **power**, and of **love**, and of a **sound mind.***

1. **Power** (dunamis) – where we derive the word dynamite; it is the Spirit's ability in us, the power of God
2. **Love** (agape) – the love of God; unselfish in its nature; the Love of God
3. **Sound Mind** (sophronismos) – self-control; equates to wisdom; the Wisdom of God

We have to decide like the parable of the Talents are we going to bury our talent in the ground or put it to use and cause it to increase. The choice is ours. If we are not living the *Abundant Life*, we certainly cannot show up before God and complain. As Christians we are intended to be prosperous, but not so we can hoard the money for ourselves.

> *St. Matthew 6:19* ***Lay not up for yourselves treasures upon earth***, *where moth and rust doth corrupt, and where thieves break through and steal:*
> *St. Matthew 6:20* ***But lay up for yourselves treasures in heaven***, *where neither moth nor rust doth corrupt, and where thieves do not break through nor steal:*

Does Jesus forbid us not to amass riches on earth? The term "Lay up", is derived from the Greek word thesaurizo (*thay-sow-rid'-zo*) meaning to heap up or to hoard (to keep to oneself). If we read Matthew 6:19 carefully, we see that Jesus does not prohibit us from gathering treasures on earth, but He warns us against accumulating them just for us. If we did not accumulate wealth on the earth how could we leave an inheritance to our families?

> *Proverbs 13:22* ***A good man leaveth an inheritance to his children's children***: *and the wealth of the sinner is laid up for the just.*

When Jesus says, "To lay up treasures in heaven," He is giving us the proper perspective concerning finances. Money is merely a means to an end. It is not the goal, just a way to reach it. Your focus should always be on your true goals. Jesus put it this way, "Where your treasure is there will your heart be also."

We consciously and unconsciously think about what we cherish the most. We will continually keep tabs on and ensure that our treasure is safe. That is why when we fall in love, all we can think about is the other person. We call and talk for hours. We cannot stand to be apart too long. This is how we are built. It is natural. God does not condemn us for continually thinking about our treasure. Quite the opposite, He advises us to cherish an eternal and lasting one, because anything else is short sighted.

So in answer to the question I asked at the beginning of the chapter. Does the Bible separate wealth from holiness? No, it does not. Wealth is a part of God's plan and blessing for all of us.

Since this is a book about how to get the abundant life and wealth is included in it; we should also look at the principles of building wealth from a biblical perspective. Wealth also follows the pattern of sowing and reaping established in scriptures.

Therefore, to build wealth we must first have a seed. The seed must then be planted in good ground. This requires our labor. If all goes well, after a period of time, we will reap a harvest. The harvest will vary in quantity, because the yield is always proportional.

So what constitutes a seed? The seed is dependent upon the produce desired. Since what we want to produce is wealth, the seed is normally our labor. I said normally because the seed could also be money. How can the seed be money, if what I am trying produce is money? If you are trying to produce apples, you need to plant apple seeds. Once you have produced some apples, you could then use the seeds within the apple to produce more. In other words, you are taking part of the produce (the seeds within) to create even more produce. In the same vein, we can use money (seed) to produce more money.

When we give our tithes or offerings are we planting seed? No, as we have already seen tithes and offerings are considered produce, not seed. We give tithes in accordance to God's Word and offerings are an expression of our gratitude for how He has blessed us. But, putting our money in the collection plate is not a form of planting. Which means it is not how we build wealth from a biblical perspective.

Hear me out. I know that sounds like blasphemy. However, look at what the Word says about it.

> *Deuteronomy 14:22* **Thou shalt truly tithe all the increase of thy seed, that the field bringeth forth** *year by year.*

The Law (first five books of the Bible) states we tithe the increase of our seed, which is our produce. So, tithes and offerings are produce (fruit) that we give to God, not seeds we plant. Why is this important? It all sounds like spiritual semantics. Malachi is normally used in reference to tithes and offerings. So, we should look at it briefly.

121

Malachi 3:8 **Will a man rob God?** *Yet ye have robbed me.* **But ye say, Wherein have we robbed thee? In tithes and offerings.**
Malachi 3:9 Ye are cursed with a curse: for ye have robbed me, even this whole nation.
Malachi 3:10 **Bring ye all the tithes into the storehouse,** *that there may be meat in mine house,* **and prove me now herewith,** *saith the LORD of hosts,* **if I will** *not open you the windows of heaven, and* **pour you out a blessing, that there shall not be room enough to receive it.**
Malachi 3:11 And **I will rebuke the devourer** *for your sakes, and* **he shall not destroy the fruits of your ground;** *neither shall your vine cast her fruit before the time in the field, saith the LORD of hosts.*

God is not blessing Israel because they are giving Him their seed. He is blessing their obedience to His commandment to tithe. Look at what happens after they give their tithes. God pours out a blessing so abundant that they will not be able to contain it all. How will He accomplish this feat? God says He will stop the devourer from destroying the fruit of our ground and from having premature fruit. Insect infestations cause's fruit to be premature, so God is saying He will stop the devourer from ruining their <u>next harvest</u>. Again why is this significant?

Here is the problem. If you mistakenly think your tithes and offerings are seed you have planted, you will naturally wait for God to give the increase. Conversely, the Lord will be waiting for you to plant some more seeds, so He can bless your subsequent harvest. This is a spiritual stalemate. Nobody wins.

How does this work out in practical terms? If you are working a nine to five job, for minimum wage and paying your tithes and offerings faithfully, you naturally expect God to bless you. In accordance to His Word, you will be the most blessed minimum wage earner, but you will certainly not be wealthy.

What you really want to do is to plant a seed that God can bless to make you wealthy. If you stay at your minimum-wage job, then your seed could take the form of applying for and taking advantage of promotional opportunities. It could take the form of investing in stocks, bonds or real estate. It might come from making a hobby a second career or possibly from patenting a new invention, etcetera. These are examples of seeds that God can bless. But, note that He is not blessing what you put in the offering plate.

If we just continue to work at our same nine to five without doing anything else, we will never see real abundance. God is not at fault here, because He will be powerless to bless us. Albert Einstein put it this way, "Insanity is doing the same thing over and over again and expecting different results."

I know there are some who declare they have received unexpected checks in the mail, due to their giving. I do not deny that God does move this way sometimes, but it is the exception rather than the rule. The fact remains nine times out of ten, you will need to plant a seed instead of waiting by the mailbox. Jesus instructed us to be wise like serpents, but as harmless as doves.[61]

We are instructed to give 10%, in order for God to bless the 90% we have left. Therefore, the seed is in the 90% still in our possession, not in the offering plate. The book of 2 Kings Chapter four is a good illustration of this principle. The story concerns a widow whose husband was a faithful prophet with Elisha. She was left in debt and the creditors were about to take her sons as payment. It is important to note in the story, God did not bless her tithes and offerings. He looked for and blessed what she had left, a pot of oil. The oil became her seed and she reaped enough to pay all her debts and live on the rest.[62] If we are not planting (investing) a portion of what we have left, how can God bless us?

The Bible describes through parables, stories and commands, how the Lord blesses His people. It is our job to understand and get inline with His Word. Do not get me wrong everyone will not become rich. The goal is not prosperity, but to increase His Kingdom. Nevertheless, everyone should not be poor.

God intends for Christians as a whole to be financially independent. How do we know that? This was His intention for Israel and it extends to His Church. In the book of Deuteronomy 28:1-15, God openly details His intention for Israel.

- Blessed in the city and field
- Blessed the fruit of your body, ground and cattle
- Increase of your kine (cows) and sheep
- Blessed is your basket and store
- Blessed coming in and going out
- Enemies to be smitten and flee 7 ways
- Blessed are your storehouses
- Blessed is everything you put your hands to do
- All people will see that you are called by God
- You will be plenteous in goods
- You will have rain in its season

- You will lend to many nations and not borrow
- You will be the head and not the tail
- You will be above and not beneath

This is how the nation of Israel was to be blessed by God, if they stayed in obedience to His Word. The apostle Paul declared that we (Christians) have obtained a better covenant than Israel, which is established on better promises (Hebrews 8:6). I do not know about you, but Israel's promises blew me away and we have better promises. Wow.

If this was not enough, God made provision for any Israelite, who was poor within the prosperous nation. Every seventh year was considered the year of release. Meaning anyone who owed money to their fellow Hebrew was free from the debt in the seventh year, even if they just incurred it in the sixth year.[63] This means that God does not want or intend for His people to remain in debt.

In a sense, whoever lends to you, reigns over you. Debt is a form of bondage. This is why Paul says, "Owe no man anything but love."[64] **Christ came to set us free. Free in all areas of our lives, not just spiritually.**

Some churches are against the prosperity message because they think it goes against holiness. God's intention for us is clear. Again, the goal is not prosperity, but it is definitely one of the blessings.

> *Deuteronomy 28:9* ***The LORD shall establish thee an holy people unto himself,*** *as he hath sworn unto thee, if thou shalt keep the commandments of the LORD thy God, and walk in his ways.*

125

Deuteronomy 28:10 **And all people of the earth shall see that thou art called by the name of the LORD**; *and they shall be afraid of thee.*

The best testimony we could ever have as Christians, is success. Nothing speaks louder. Talk is cheap. In other words, we can witness all day long, but "the proof is in the pudding." **God always intended for us to draw the nations to Him via the blessings He bestows upon us and of course love.** God prospers us spiritually, mentally and physically.

Abundant living is one of the believer's most powerful witnesses for Christ and it has been neglected for far too long. It is the demonstration of God's power in us. Start living the *Abundant Life* today.

Robert

Your brother in Christ

About the Author

Robert R. Davis is the Assistant Pastor of New Life Worship Center in West Haven, Connecticut. He is a gifted teacher of the Word, dedicated to pursuing and sharing the full knowledge of Christ.

In addition to this work Robert Davis has written:

The Final Message:
Understanding the Book of Revelation

6 Things Every Christian Should Know:
The Fundamentals of Christianity

What Lies Within:
Understanding the Holy Spirit

To order books by Robert R. Davis or to contact the author, visit his website at **http://www.robertrdavis.com**.

The Final Message

Understanding the Book of Revelation

Robert R. Davis

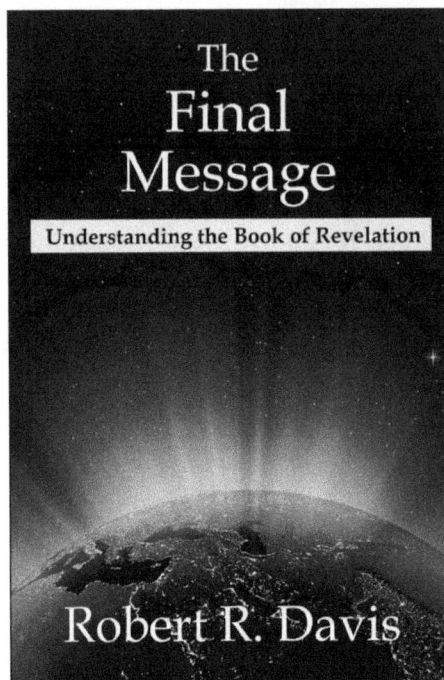

ISBN: 978-0-9797469-0-1

What makes *The Final Message* any different from the hundreds of books before it? Most books on Revelation rehash traditional interpretations with only slight variations. This work checks every vision and theory against the Bible. The Holy Scriptures are the barometer to determine whether the findings are fact or fiction. Any interpretation that cannot be verified through scripture will be disallowed, no matter how long it has been revered. Every vision is scrutinized against the rest of the Bible in order to glean its true meaning. The result is an interpretation that harmonizes perfectly with the whole Bible. You will walk away wondering why you did not see these truths before.

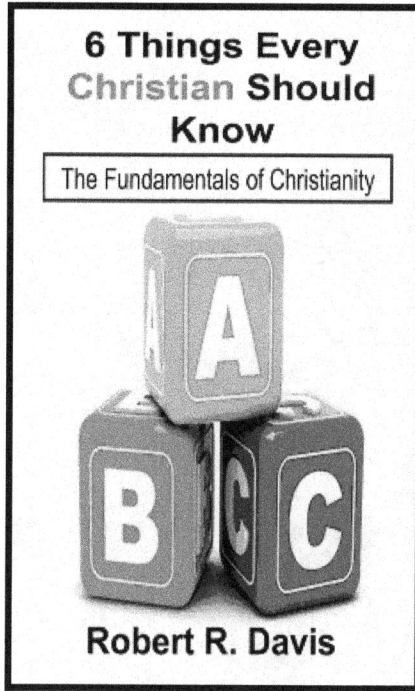

6 Things Every Christian Should Know

The Fundamentals of Christianity

Robert R. Davis

ISBN: 978-0-9797469-3-2

The book of Hebrews chapter six is the basis for this work. In it, the apostle Paul outlined what he considered the foundational truths every Christian should know. Therefore, these teachings should be the first lessons a new believer receives in the Church. Unfortunately, most Christians never receive this fundamental instruction and so attempt to build their faith without a proper foundation.

This book will not only tell you the meaning of these principles, but it explains how and why they are tied together. Insightful, fresh and reverent, it is a must have for every believer.

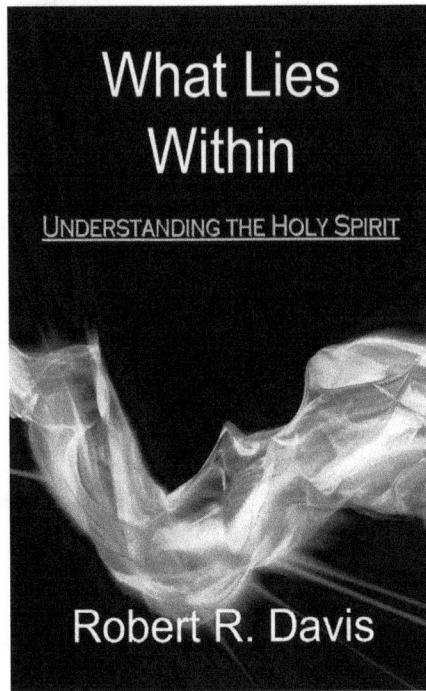

What Lies
Within

UNDERSTANDING THE HOLY SPIRIT

Robert R. Davis

ISBN: 978-0-9797469-1-8

The Holy Ghost is the long awaited promise of the Father, through which all believers receive the power of God. Even the apostles of Jesus needed this unique gift before they could be sent out as witnesses. Therefore, I believe it is imperative that we have a firm understanding of the Spirit and how He pertains to our lives today.

The Holy Spirit is literally the breath of God. But, the Spirit is more than an unseen force that gives life. The Holy Spirit is the very essence or nature of God. This is why we can call God our Father and not just our creator. He has placed His nature inside of us via His Spirit. Understand for yourself the power and purpose of what lies within.

References:

[1] Holy Bible. Romans 13:8-9.

[2] Holy Bible. 1 Corinthians 13:13.

[3] Quinn, Daniel. 2 August 2010. Law of Life. < http://en.wikipedia.org/wiki/Law_of_Life>

[4] Holy Bible. St. Matthew 5:44

[5] Holy Bible. Genesis 1:11-12.

[6] Holy Bible. Galatians 5:16.

[7] Holy Bible. 1 Peter 4:17.

[8] Holy Bible. Romans 10:17.

[9] Holy Bible. St. John 15:8.

[10] Davis, Robert. 6 Things Every Christian Should Know: The Fundamentals of Christianity (Connecticut: Kingdom Works Publishing, 2009) p. 34-35.

[11] Holy Bible. Romans 12:2.

[12] Holy Bible. Psalms 139:14.

[13] Hill, Napoleon and Kimbro, Dennis. Think and Grow Rich a Black Choice. (New York: Fawcett Crest, 1991) p20.

[14] Holy Bible. St. Matthew 13:10-16.

[15] Ruiz, Don Miguel. The Four Agreements: A Practical Guide to Personal Freedom (California: Amber-Allen Publishing, 1997) p. 26-27.

[16] Holy Bible. Galatians 6:9.

[17] Holy Bible. 2 Corinthians 5:17.

[18] Doidge, Norman. M.D. The Brain that changes Itself: Stories of Personal Triumph from the Frontiers of Brain Science (Penguin Books, 2007) p. 169.

[19] Merzinich, Michael, Ph. D. 16 April 2008. On the Brain. About Brain Plasticity. < http://merzenich.positscience.com/?page_id=143>

[20] Holy Bible. Proverbs 23:7.

[21] Association for Psychological Science. 2 June 2011. Depression and Negative Thoughts. <http://www.psychologicalscience.org/index.php/news/releases/depression-and-negative-thoughts.html>

[22] Holy Bible. St. Matthew 11:28-30.

[23] It's now a proven fact your unconscious mind is running your life. <http://www.lifetrainings.com/Your-unconscious-mind-is-running-you-life.html>

[24] <http://www.lifetrainings.com/Your-unconscious-mind-is-running-you-life.html>

[25] Ariely, Dan, Professor. 29 January 2008. How Honest People Cheat. <http://blogs.hbr.org/cs/2008/01/how_honest_people_cheat.html>

[26] Thompson, Curt. Neurons that fire together wire together. <http://www.beingknown.com/2010/07/neurons-that-fire-together-wire-together/>

[27] Davis. 6 Things Every Christian Should Know. P. 40-41.

[28] Holy Bible. St. Luke 18:1.

[29] Holy Bible. Deuteronomy 28:13.

[30] Holy Bible. St. Matthew 5:13-14.

[31] Holy Bible. Proverbs 13:12.

[32] Holy Bible. St. John 16:24.

[33] Holy Bible. Malachi 3:10.

[34] Holy Bible. Acts 10:34.

[35] Holy Bible. James 1:14-15.

[36] Holy Bible. St. John 16:33.

[37] Holy Bible. Acts 14:22.

[38] Holy Bible. St. Luke 6:45.

[39] Holy Bible. Proverbs 18:21.

[40] Holy Bible. Romans 10:17.

[41] Davis, Robert. The Final Message: Understanding the Book of Revelation (Connecticut: Kingdom Works Publishing, 2008) p. 4.

[42] Holy Bible. St. Matthew 6:33.

[43] Holy Bible. Ecclesiastes 10:19.

[44] Holy Bible. Proverbs 4:7.

[45] Holy Bible. Genesis 2:18.

[46] Holy Bible. 1 John 2:16.

[47] Holy Bible. 2 Timothy 2:15.

[48] Holy Bible. Romans 8:31.

[49] Holy Bible. Hebrews 11:6.

[50] Holy Bible. St. Matthew 18:19.

[51] Holy Bible. James 1:7-8.

[52] Smith, William L. The Human Electromagnetic Energy Field: Its Relationship to Interpersonal Communication. <http://citeseerx.ist.psu.edu/viewdoc/summary?doi=10.1.1.10.26>

[53] Davis. The Final Message. p. 5.

[54] Holy Bible. Job 1:21.

[55] Longely, Robert. Lifetime Earnings Soar with Education. 13 Feb 2010.
<http://usgovinfo.about.com/od/moneymatters/a/edandearnings.htm>
[56] Jamal, Azim and McKinnon, Harvey. The Power of Giving: How Giving Back Enriches Us All (New York: Tarcher/Penguin, 2005) p. 68.
[57] Holy Bible. Isaiah 9:7.
[58] Holy Bible. 2 Timothy 2:15.
[59] Hill and Kimbro. Think and Grow Rich. p 256-257.
[60] Trump, Donald and Kiyosaki, Robert. Why we want You to be Rich: Two Men, One Message (Rich Press, 2007) p. 51.
[61] Holy Bible. St. Matthew 10:16.
[62] Holy Bible. 2 Kings 4:1-7.
[63] Holy Bible. Deuteronomy 15:1-2.
[64] Holy Bible. Romans 13:8.

www.ingramcontent.com/pod-product-compliance
Lightning Source LLC
Chambersburg PA
CBHW060941040426
42445CB00011B/954